Dainty Dining

Dainty Dining

Vintage recipes, memories and memorabilia
from America's department store tea rooms

Angela Webster McRae

Dainty Dining: Vintage recipes, memories and memorabilia from America's
department store tea rooms

Copyright © 2011 by Angela Webster McRae

ISBN 978-0-615-53345-2

Library of Congress Control Number: 2011916880

Vintage memorabilia depicted in this book is from the collection of the author.

Except where otherwise noted, all other images are by the author.

Cover and Book Design: Deberah Williams.

On the cover: Rich's Magnolia Room Chicken Salad Amandine, Frozen Fruit Salad and
Cheese Straws.

Dedication

To my wonderful parents,

Buren and Nancy Webster

Truly, I thank my God upon every remembrance of you! (Phillipians 1:3)

Acknowledgments

If I hadn't started writing the Tea With Friends blog in 2007, I might not have written this book. I would certainly never have met some of the wonderful women in the tea community here in the U.S. and around the world. My fellow tea bloggers in particular have been a great source of friendship and encouragement, especially Bernideen Canfield, Teresa Carter, Linda Jennings, Lynn Karegeannes, Marilyn Miller, Nancy Reppert, Maureen Rogers and Stephanie Wilson. Tea educator and writer Phyllis Barkey has been a great encouragement as well. Thank you all for teaching me there is always more to learn about teatime!

Of course I would not be a student of tea today had I not learned to love the beverage, the ritual and the tea party thanks to a host of tea-loving girlfriends. Liz Barnett, Beth Blair, Sandra Blair, Kathy Bohannon, Nikki Brimer and Ruth Schroeder have created tea memories with me for many years now. And while Ashly Camp and Susan West have also shared tea with me, it's their influence in the important areas of baking and shopping for which I am most grateful!

I am so very fortunate to be able to work with my dear friend (and fellow tea-lover) Deberah Williams, whose design talents make everything I touch look about a thousand times better than they would otherwise.

And finally, my sweet husband Alex McRae is my greatest encourager, in writing and in life, and he also served as chief taste-tester for the foods appearing in this book. I think the man deserves a steak, don't you?

Contents

Introduction

My mother used to tell people I was born in a dressing room at Rich's Department Store. I've seen my birth certificate and it lists Crawford Long Hospital in Atlanta as my birthplace, but I loved Rich's and certainly didn't mind being associated with that late, great store.

When I was growing up, Rich's was where my family went whenever we needed "good" clothes or "nice" gifts. It was the gold standard of stores in Georgia, a place whose very name meant quality. My Christmas gifts for junior high teachers were often costume jewelry brooches chosen from the piles that glittered on displays in the center aisles at Rich's.

My high school wardrobe was often selected from the junior department at Rich's, and in college I bought my first department store makeup at their elegantly styled makeup counters. When I graduated, Rich's handed me my first credit card.

Because I was born the very last year of the Baby Boom, 1964, that meant I was not limited to a single downtown department store location since Rich's, like so many of its retailing peers across the nation, was by then expanding into the suburbs. My favorite Rich's location was not the flagship store in downtown Atlanta but rather the Cobb Center store near my grandmother's home in Marietta.

After I graduated from college and moved to Newnan, Georgia, the nearest Rich's store was a mere 20-minute interstate trip away in Union City. As a newly-employed journalist furnishing my first apartment, I found my first bedroom ensemble and my first dishes at Rich's. The store continued to loom large in my retail life, but it was also to intersect with my professional life on several occasions.

In 1989, the movie *Gone With the Wind* celebrated its 50th anniversary and I had the happy assignment of covering the cast reunion held at the downtown Atlanta Rich's store.

A decade later, I was again at Rich's on a newspaper assignment. This time the Rich's location was North Point Mall in Alpharetta and the visitor was Sarah,

Duchess of York, who was there to promote a new line of Wedgwood dishes. The duchess charmed the crowd by showing the custom made Asprey train case designed to protect her teawares, including the Wedgwood teapot which was a wedding gift from the company to her and Prince Andrew.

The Duchess was quite fond of her tea, and so am I. For several years I wrote a newspaper column called Tea With Friends. In 2007 I began to write a web log, or blog, of the same name. Blogs were still somewhat new then, and I hadn't realized people from outside my usual circle of readers might care what I had to say about tea.

The loveliest people came into my life through this blog, many of whom I suspect will remain lifelong friends. Face to face, I met a successful local caterer who shares my love of tea, a fellow tea-loving quilter in a nearby town, and a talented artist and tea lover from North Carolina who gave me my first tea plant. In fall of 2010, a delightful woman from South Carolina came to my town with several fun friends in tow just to have tea with me in a local tea room!

By way of the internet I met a young father who works on a tea plantation in Darjeeling, India and a stylish young mother in Istanbul, Turkey who is raising her beautiful daughter to love teatime. A kindred spirit in Honolulu, Hawaii endeared herself to me when she sent a recipe for Japanese Potato Salad Tea Sandwiches. Closer to home, a fellow fabric-lover in North Carolina has often shared tea samples and tea-themed-fabric-shopping advice. And when I started mentioning my interest in department store tea rooms, a kindhearted tea friend in Michigan began to share information and encouragement. If you want to meet the world's nicest group of people, explore the world of tea!

One day on the blog, I shared a photo of a Limoges porcelain teacup I'd found. It had a bow for a handle and was marked "John Wanamaker, Philadelphia." As a lifelong shopper I knew the Wanamaker name, but I learned Wanamaker's was also the home of the Great Crystal Tea Room and decided I wanted to learn more about the man and his store. I also asked my blog readers where they had shopped and dined, and soon I received comments and e-mails. Burdines in Miami. Hess's in Allentown, Pennsylvania. Younker Brothers in Des Moines, Iowa. And, of course, the Magnolia Room at Rich's in Atlanta.

What a fun time I've had trying to unearth recipes and stories and memorabilia from all these great stores and their tea rooms and restaurants, many of them now just a memory. I see this book as a sort of travel guide to stores I've (for the most part) never visited and tea rooms I've never dined in. I've recreated dishes I never ate and conjured memories that aren't even mine.

Yet I believe there is value in attempting a look back. A lifelong interest in antiques and collecting means I have learned to love the past, and my tea friends tell me the same thing. We are high-fiving each other when one finds a tea trivet for 50 cents at an estate sale, or when someone's mother passes down a treasured family teapot. There's something about these old things that speaks to many of us.

Looking back at the store founders, I was impressed with their commitment to quality goods and customer satisfaction. I loved learning about John Wanamaker and how he wandered into his restaurant's kitchen to inspect the food. I admire how Marshall Field in Chicago overcame so many obstacles on his road to becoming a retail legend. It was inspiring to learn that my own beloved Rich's once helped the Atlanta public schools meet their payroll.

I also received a crash course in retail history and learned, for instance, that stores in the early days did not use cash registers. Some stores had little payment baskets that shuttled back and forth on pulleys over the heads of customers, transporting payments to one central location. By the forties, newfangled pneumatic tubes like the ones at my bank's drive-through window were whipping payments from floor to floor in half a minute or less.

Department stores were often first in their community to embrace new technologies such as air conditioning, escalators and revolving doors. All this was impressive, but what charmed me most were stories of the tea rooms and restaurants that opened in these stores.

Years ago, I read a newspaper article titled "Dainty Dining" which reflected on the era of the department store tea room and how the foods were often described as dainty, or perhaps were served in dainty portions. I began to look for recipes from some of America's great department stores. Most of the stores in this book eventually opened other branches, but I chose to focus largely on the flagship stores.

While I certainly enjoyed learning about America's retail history and how it shaped popular culture in the late 19th and early 20th centuries, I never aimed to become a department store scholar or even an expert on tea rooms. I still have much to learn about these places.

My interest was simply in finding out the answer to the one question we ask of anyone who has been on a trip to someplace we'd like to go: Did you eat anything good?

The answer is a resounding yes!

The Art Deco Bullock's Wilshire store opened in 1929. An earlier version of the store is shown opposite.

BULLOCK'S, LOS ANGELES.　　　95982

Bullock's Wilshire
Los Angeles, California

The driver pulls up near the motor court of Bullock's Wilshire, the Art Deco department store whose tower marks the sky some 241 feet above Wilshire Boulevard in Los Angeles. The platinum blonde in the back seat makes no move to alight from the car, however. Oh, she's here to shop all right and fully intends to see some designer dresses today, she just doesn't plan on stepping inside the store. When you're Mae West, you see, you don't even have to get out of the limousine. When you're Mae West, the store comes to you.

I t's the store where some of the biggest names in Hollywood came to see and be seen. You might say the building itself is something of a celebrity, since Bullock's Wilshire has appeared in Cary Grant's *Topper* (1937) and, more recently, *Bugsy* (1991) and *The Aviator* (2004).

This architectural celebrity's bio began in 1907 when John Gillespie Bullock and Percy Glen Winnet opened a store in downtown Los Angeles. The two had worked for Arthur Letts Sr., owner of a store called The Broadway, and convinced him to finance their new store aimed at more upscale shoppers. Eventually Bullock and Winnet were able to buy out Lett's interest in the store. In 1929 they opened their magnificent Art Deco palace on Wilshire Boulevard.

The building's design was praised from the day it opened, and rightly so. From the terra cotta facade to the marbled, mirrored and lighted sales floors to the copper, bronze and gunmetal elevator doors, Bullock's Wilshire was a shrine to modern

Vintage postcards show the foyer and tea room at Bullock's in the 1920s.

design. It was also one of the first stores built with the automobile in mind. Its motor court's ceiling even featured a frescoed mural with a transportation theme.

Judy Garland, Greta Garbo, Doris Day and John Wayne are among the famous faces who shopped at Bullock's. The Duke was a frequent guest of the fifth floor tea room, where he came to dine and see the fashion models.

Former First Lady Pat Nixon, June Lockhart and Angela Lansbury all worked at Bullock's at one time. Years later, when Lansbury returned to the store to shoot episodes of *Murder She Wrote,* she was presented a sterling silver sugar and creamer from the store's tea room.

In 1934, a California woman wrote a guidebook for visitors and described the atmosphere in the Bullock's Wilshire tea room:

"The Desert Tea Room on the Fifth floor is the rendezvous for every body. The day we were last there, Gloria Swanson, closely squired by her latest fancy, Herbert Marshall, wasn't even creating a flutter. The employees are so used to this sort of thing, you see. By the way, this tea room is something you must be sure to visit. The desert motif is so very restful and the copper cactus on the window grating sets the tempo, which is so well carried out that even the slats on the

This undated menu cover from Bullock's Tea Room features an elegant bouquet of roses.

Venetian blinds are painted alternately in pink and green and ivory to keep the decor!"

The store was much more than just a tea room and celebrities, however. *The Great Merchants* notes that "there was little that Bullock's would not do for a customer." Late one Saturday, the night watchman took a call from a tearful customer upset that a china order had not arrived in time for the golden wedding anniversary it was supposed to celebrate the next day. Calls were made, the gift was found, and the next morning a store executive delivered the china himself.

One Christmas, a store employee overheard a conversation about a widowed mother whose children's gifts "from Santa" had arrived too early and been discovered by the children. The store sent along some new gifts "from Santa" for free.

The store closed in 1993. While many of the great department stores exist now only in shoppers' memories, Bullock's Wilshire's magnificent Art Deco building today serves as the law school and library for Southwestern Law School.

Some future stars of the legal world may inhabit its halls today, but there was a time when the glitz and glamour that was old Hollywood shopped and dined at the architectural star of Wilshire Boulevard.

Bullock's Oriental Chicken Salad

This recipe was a reader request printed in the Los Angeles Times *in 1984, shared with the newspaper by the chef at Bullock's. One of the more modern-era tea room recipes I've tried, this salad is hearty, crunchy and attractive. Flavored with soy and Worcestershire sauces, the dressing is rich in flavor and unique in a tea room dish.*

1 (6-3/4-ounce) package rice sticks (find in the ethnic foods
section of the grocery store)
Oil for deep-frying
1 head of lettuce, chopped
3 cups diced or shredded cooked chicken
6 tablespoons sliced almonds, lightly toasted

Dressing:

2 cups mayonnaise
1-1/4 teaspoons Worcestershire sauce
2 teaspoons soy sauce
2 teaspoons oil
1 tablespoon plus 1 teaspoon prepared mustard
1/8 teaspoon lemon juice

Deep-fry rice sticks, a small handful at a time, in hot oil 1 to 2 minutes or until puffed. They should sizzle and pop almost immediately, and you don't want them to get too brown. Drain on paper towels. For dressing, combine mayonnaise, Worcestershire sauce, soy sauce, oil, mustard and lemon juice and stir. Makes about 2 cups.

For each serving, place 1 cup chopped lettuce on plate. Add dressing (a tablespoon or two, as desired) and toss. Add a handful of cooked rice sticks, then top with 1/2 cup chicken and 1 tablespoon of the almonds. Yields 6 servings.

$\mathcal{B}urdines$
Miami, Florida

No wonder people love to read old restaurant menus. Take the one from Saturday, June 14, 1952 from Burdines Hibiscus Tea Room in Miami. Bright red hibiscus blossoms on the cover are set against a tropical green background. "Welcome Shriners" it says on the back, advising Mr. and Mrs. Shriner where to find Florida souvenirs (gift bar, street floor), U-Ask-It stations (throughout store, near escalator landings) or the Beauty Salon (third floor). Inside, the menu lists such sunny selections as Freshly Pressed Orange or Grapefruit Juice (15 cents), A Dozen Fresh Florida Jumbo Shrimps in a Sunshine Bowl of Cracked Ice, Center of Cocktail Sauce, Lemon Wedge (one dollar) and Fresh Orange Icebox Pie with Orange Sauce (25 cents).

Sunshine, Shriners and Shrimp. What a great store!

Today Miami is known as one of the busiest cruise ship ports in the world, the home of singer Gloria Estefan and the Miami Heat pro basketball team. A little more than a hundred years ago, however, Miami was just a small fishing village when retired Confederate Army General William Burdine decided to open a dry goods company here.

Ever wondered what the term "dry goods" means? The book *The Grand Emporiums* sums it up nicely: "Dry goods stores take their name from shops run by New England merchants, many of whom were shipowners and direct importers in colonial times. Their two chief imports were rum and bolts of calico, which were traditionally carried on opposite sides of the store—a 'wet goods' side containing the

Tea-loving customers ordering off this Burdines menu from June 14, 1952 could get a pot of Orange Pekoe, English Breakfast, Ceylon, Darjeeling, Oolong or Green Tea for 15 cents. Iced tea was 10 cents.

rum and a 'dry goods' side holding the calico. 'Wet goods' disappeared from the language, though the taste for same certainly didn't abate, but stores that sell piece goods, and even some small town department stores, are still occasionally called dry goods stores."

Burdine and his son John opened a dry goods store in 1898 with just $300. They offered a small selection of clothes and notions that were sold mainly to construction workers, Spanish-American War soldiers, and the local Miccosukee and Seminole Native Americans, who paid with money they had earned from the sale of alligator and otter skins.

As Florida's population soared, the Burdines reputation soared right along with it. By 1912 it was a full-scale department store, and Miami had become a tourist destination for northerners escaping the cold winters. When the founder died, son Roddey became manager and emphasized fashion and the store's tropical location. It was Roddey who coined the term "Sunshine Fashions" for Burdines.

In 1940, the store had a surprise visit from the Duke of Windsor. Roberta Morgan describes the visit in her book *It's Better at Burdines*: "The former King of England was accompanied in the store by his bodyguard. ... They managed to get as far as the fifth floor as they searched for an electric tea kettle, before a mob of customers and sales girls surrounded them. They were quickly rescued, in expert Burdines' style, by the store's general manager, who gave them sanctuary from the crowd in his private office. He then called in buyers and department heads to display all the merchandise the Duke was seeking—ties, sport shirts, a thermos ice bucket, silver salt and pepper shakers, and a novelty cup and spoon. ... Later that same day, at his request, Burdines sent armloads of clothing to the Wenner-Gren yacht, where Sunshine Fashions were displayed for the Duchess in one stateroom, while the Duke selected more clothing in another."

Burdines always played up its "Florida store" image in decor and promotional materials, and that included the Hibiscus Tea Room. One vintage postcard shows a teal and peach decor. The back of the card reads, "With adjacent 'Men Only' Grille ... the delightfully air-conditioned place for Florida Fare, served in a tropical setting ... Luncheon, Monday night Dinner, and Candlelight Tea during resort season."

Joanie Anderson remembers the "resort season" in Miami. She lives in Georgia now, but as a young girl she lived in Miami where she saw pictures in the newspaper of northern "Snowbirds" walking around Miami Beach wearing fur coats while the temperature was in the 70s or 80s!

"I remember when I saw those photos, thinking, 'Wow, wouldn't that be neat to walk around Miami Beach like that?'" Anderson said. "I also remember my parents, who had moved to Florida from Boston, Mass., telling us 'The last thing you want to wear around Miami Beach is a fur coat!'"

Anderson also has fond memories of visiting the Hibiscus Tea Room as a girl.

Going to Burdines meant dressing up, for one thing, because Burdines "was 'the Word' for the finest in fashion, jewelry, housewares ... really 'top of the line' items," Anderson said.

As a girl of just 6 or 7, Anderson ordered what became the tea room's signature dessert for girls, the Snow Princess.

"The Snow Princess dessert is memorable," Anderson said, "a cloud of fluffy, white whipped cream made up the skirt, all being 'watched over' by the beautiful Snow Princess doll, gracefully atop." She remembers everyone oohing and aahing when the dessert was brought to the table. "It was usually someone's birthday, and the servers went out of their way to make it all so special!"

Burdines stores, including the downtown Miami store, were converted to Macy's in 2005.

To this day, readers write to the *Miami Herald* sharing recollections of the Hibiscus Tea Room and its royal dessert for little girls.

The Snow Princess

The porcelain dolls originally featured atop the Snow Princess aren't widely available today, but an inexpensive substitute can be found in the toy aisle of your local dollar store. Craft websites such as Etsy.com also sell doll head "picks" which can be used as toppers for today's Snow Princess desserts.

Ingredients:

Vanilla ice cream
1 pint heavy whipping cream, whipped with 1 tablespoon of confectioners' sugar
Silver dragees

Place one well-rounded scoop of vanilla ice cream in center of a saucer or serving dish. Add a second scoop of ice cream and insert doll figure or doll head. (If using entire doll, raise her sweet little hands before decorating and lower when completed.) Pipe whipped cream in rows to form a skirt for the doll. I used a star tip, but other shapes could also be used. When the princess is fully "dressed" with whipped cream, embellish her skirt with silver dragees.

Home of The Denver Dry Goods Co.
The Largest Store in the Central West
400 Feet Long—Seven Acres Floor Area
1,200 Employes—A $1,500,000 Stock
15th to 16th on California Street
Denver, Colorado.

Denver Dry Goods
Denver, Colorado

For rent: Amazing luxury loft in the heart of downtown Denver, Colorado. Centrally located near 16th Street Mall, Colorado Convention Center, Pepsi Center and Denver Performing Arts Center. Amenities include high ceilings, newly refinished hardwood floors and freshly painted walls. Also available: fitness center, private parking and rooftop jacuzzi with breathtaking view of the Denver skyline. And did we mention that on quiet evenings, if you listen very closely, you can hear salesgirls of the 1950s ringing up dress purchases of shoppers on their way to the fifth floor tea room for a lunch of Chicken a la King, Lemon Meringue Pie and a pot of Earl Grey Tea?

That last line is pure conjecture, but it doesn't mean it isn't true.

A 2011 listing by a Denver real estate firm did indeed advertise the basic information about the Downtown Denver Loft that was available, but only a reference to the "Historic Denver Dry Goods Building" alluded to the structure's storied past.

This wouldn't be the first time part of the former department store would become someone's new home. In 2007, the *Denver Post* reported that the old tea room in the Denver Dry Goods building, "one of the premier lofts in downtown Denver," had sold for nearly $2.7 million. The buyer was a local attorney, whose family planned to make the 4,000-square-foot loft their new home.

"It's an unbelievable, beautiful property," the new owner told the *Post*, calling the property "an iconic treasure of historic downtown Denver."

Mike McPhee of the *Denver Post* wrote, "During downtown Denver's heyday following WWII, eating lunch at the Tea Room was a proud tradition, almost a rite of passage, for many Denverites. Mothers and daughters wore white gloves and strings of pearls, to be served by white-aproned waitresses bringing warm plates of chicken a la king or prime rib and mashed potatoes covered under gleaming silver domes."

It was founded as the McNamara Dry Goods Company, but a change in ownership and a change in name came by the time a new building went up in 1889 and was named Denver Dry Goods. A postcard from 1915 boasted that the store was "The Largest Store in the Central West—400 Feet Long—Seven Acres Floor Area—1,200 employes (sic)—A $1,500,000 Stock." The store even sold its own brand of horse saddles called Powder River Saddles.

Denver Dry Goods was Denver's premier retail store for more than 50 years. When the store closed and the tea room served its last meals in 1987, preservationists feared the building was in danger of being demolished. Community leaders made sure that didn't happen.

The Denver Dry Goods Building stands today as a mixed-use development in the heart of downtown Denver. It includes affordable and market rate housing, market rate condominiums, offices and retail stores.

Hopefully, some of the new tenants know how to make Chicken a la King!

Chicken a la King

"The Denver," as the Denver Dry Goods tea room was known, liked to serve this dish in puff pastry shells with a chicken cut-out on top, but it may also be served over rice, as I prefer mine.

2 sticks butter
1-1/2 cups flour
8 cups chicken stock (canned is fine)
1 cup half-and-half
1 pound cooked, boneless chicken breasts, diced
1 large red bell pepper, cut in 1/4-inch strips
1 large green bell pepper, cut in 1/4-inch strips
1/2 pound sliced mushrooms, sautéed in butter
Salt and white pepper (to taste)

Melt butter in large saucepan. Whisk in flour, cooking over medium heat a few minutes. Gradually add chicken stock, continuing to whisk. Cook over medium heat and continue to whisk until thickened. Stir in half-and-half. Cook over low heat for about 25 minutes. Add more chicken stock, depending on desired consistency, then add remaining ingredients. Cook over low heat about 20 minutes. I am a cook who is a light salter, so I put only a small amount of salt and pepper in the pot, preferring to season portions individually afterward. Yields 8-10 servings.

Shell Fish

Lobster Cocktail	75	Oyster Stew	50	Bluepoint Oysters	35—Cocktail 40
Crab Meat Cocktail	75	Cream of Oyster Stew	60	Cape Oysters	35—Cocktail 40
Fried Clams	60	Fried Oysters	70	Little Neck Clams	35—Cocktail 40
Sea Food Cocktail	75			Cherry Stone Clams	40—Cocktail 45

Relishes

Fruit Cocktail	35-65	Tomato Ketchup		Mixed Pickles	20
Celery	40	Chili Sauce A 1 Sauce		Stuffed Olives	25
Radishes	15	Fruit Coupe Filene	50	Queen Olives	20
Half of Chilled Grapefruit	30	Sliced Tomatoes or Cucumbers	35		

Soups

Puree of Green Split Peas	25	*Clam Chowder	25	Chicken Broth	25

Fish

Broiled Codfish Steak, Baked Potato	65	Fresh Shrimps Newburg on Toast, Peas	75
Boiled Deep Sea Flounder Hollandaise	70	Fried Native Smelts, *Tartare Sauce, Fried Potatoes	85
Fried Filets of Sole, *Tartare Sauce	70	Fried Scallops, *Tartare Sauce, Creamed Potatoes	95

Entrees

*Ragout of Beef en Casserole	65	Veal Cutlets Breaded Milanaise, Green Salad	75
Chicken a la Creme on Toasted Muffin	70	Braised Home Cured Ham with Spinach	80

Roasts

Roast Prime Ribs of Beef, Pan Gravy	75	Roast Stuffed Chicken, Cranberry Sauce	1.15

Vegetables

Vegetable Luncheon 70   Fresh Artichokes Hollandaise 50   New Brussels Sprouts 30

Boiled Potatoes	10	Fried Sweet Potatoes	25	Buttered Beets	20	Lima Beans	25
Boiled Sweet Potato	15	Grilled Sweet Potato	30	Fresh Spinach	35	Asparagus Tips on Toast	40
Mashed Potato	15	New String Beans	30	Fried Egg Plant	30	Corn in Cream	25
Baked Potato	15	Onions in Cream	35	Green Peas	25	New Cauliflower in Cream	40
French Fried Potatoes	20	Broiled Tomatoes	50	New Squash	25		

Salads

Fresh Mint Jelly, Celery and Tomato Salad 70

Chicken	85	Tomato	50	Mixed Fruit	75
Lobster	1.25	Cucumber	50	Celery, Apple and Nut	65
Sea Food	1.00	Stuffed Egg and Sardine	50	Egg Salad	60
Shrimp	75	Hearts of Lettuce	50	Tomato and Cucumber	50
Fresh Crab (all Claw Meat)	1.00	Combination Salad Filene	85	Cooked Fresh Vegetable Salad	75
Fresh Crab (Body Meat)	75	Chicken and Vegetable Salad Filene 1.25			

With Meat or Fish Orders only, Small Lettuce or Mixed Green Salad 30
Russian, Thousand Island or Roquefort Cheese Dressing served with Salads 15c. extra

Sandwiches

Chicken	50	Lobster Salad	75	Special Open Club	65
Chicken Salad	55	Toasted Lobster Salad	80	Pimento and Cream Cheese	30
Chicken Salad Roll	55	Lobster Club	85	Cucumber and Lettuce	40
Toasted Chicken Fricassee	75	Lobster Salad Roll	75		

Cold Meats

Cold Roast Beef	75	Cold Sliced Chicken, Light and Dark Meat	90	Cold Ham, Potato Salad	75
		Cold Sliced Chicken, All White Meat	1.00		

Cooked to Order

(Ready)

Plain Omelet	55	Spanish Omelet	75
Poached Eggs on Toast	55	Eggs au Gratin Florentine	75
Eggs Scrambled	60	Eggs Benedict	80

*Chicken Pie Family Style with Vegetables 75
Chicken Pie (all White Meat) 90

Shell Fish

Broiled Live Lobster	1.75	Broiled Chicken Lobster	1.25

Lobster, Newburg (1) 2.00   (2) 3.50

Steaks, Chops and Chicken

Sirloin Steak (1) 1.25	(2) 2.00	(3) 3.00	Lamb Chop, each	45
Tenderloin Steak (1) 1.25	(2) 2.00	(3) 3.00	Chicken a la King (1) 1.50 (2)	2.50
(Steaks Planked 50 cts. per person extra)			Broiled Spring Chicken (half) 1.35 (whole)	2.65

*Indicates articles containing Onions or Chives

Boston Post Road

Filene's

Boston

LEE HERO

THE NEW FILENE STORE,
BOSTON, U. S. A.

Filene's

Boston, Massachusetts

Hordes of women are lined up and ready to roll the moment the store opens.

The dresses they've longed for are about to go on sale, and they don't intend to miss out. They've been waiting, some of them, for years to find one of these dresses, and who knows how long it will be before such a bargain-grabbing opportunity comes again.

Soon the doors open, the crowd begins to move, and the rush is on.

Within seconds, all the dresses have been grabbed from the racks.

Sound familiar? If you think this is a description of the famous "Running of the Brides" at Filene's Basement, you're close, you're just off by a few decades ...

In 1940, a fashion buyer for Filene's in Boston managed to pull off a fashion coup for the ages by picking up some 400 Parisian dresses during World War II. *The Great Merchants* tells it this way:

"As the Germans approached Paris in 1940, buyers for Filene's basement picked up four hundred of the latest dresses by Schiaparelli, Lelong, Chanel and other famous couturiers and shipped them out through Spain. A week after Paris fell, the basement announced a sale of the dresses, normally priced at several hundred dollars, for $11 to $49 each. Fifteen thousand women were on hand when the doors opened. Within sixty seconds, every dress was off the racks. Fifteen minutes later all had been sold."

Today history repeats itself with Filene's annual Running of the Brides. Would-be brides in search of a wedding dress—some still in search of a husband—camp out before dawn for the chance to run screaming into the store and grab possible wedding dresses at rock bottom prices.

Store founder William Filene was born in 1830 to a Polish ribbon merchant. Filene emigrated first to England and then to the U.S., where he worked as a tailor in Boston. In 1881 he and his sons opened a small shop there. Ten years later, he turned over management of the store to Lincoln and Edward, the two of his four sons who showed the most talent for retailing.

Edward is credited with creating the concept of the "automatic bargain basement" method of pricing. Though other stores had basement retail areas known for their bargain prices, at Filene's a customer never had to wonder when the next markdown would occur. Basement goods were automatically marked down 25 percent after 12 selling days, another 25 percent after 18 days, a third 25 percent after 24 days, and after 30 days items were donated to local charities.

Filene's Basement stores are located nationwide, and the flagship Filene's store (now closed but undergoing renovation) was located on Washington Street in Boston. The store had a restaurant, tea room and cafe on the top floor and a lunch room and soda fountain in the basement. Jan Whitaker's *Service and Style* says that Filene's at one time held an annual children's tea party on the eighth floor, and tea dancing was a popular pastime in the tea room around 1919.

Filene's had quite a few famous faces associated with its store. Louis D. Brandeis, an attorney for Filene's, later served on the U.S. Supreme Court. One of the promising young men trained at Filene's was Frank B. Gilbreth, the famed motion-study specialist who figured prominently in his son's book *Cheaper by the Dozen.*

And if there was ever a store that knew a thing or two about what was cheaper by the dozen, or the hundred, it was Filene's.

This vintage postcard shows "a section of the Public Restaurant in the Filene Store, Boston."

Filene's Seafood Newburg

The Yankee Cook Book, *where I found this recipe, recommends you serve this dish hot on toast or in a chafing dish. I had mine plain and loved it! For an elegant presentation, serve in individual petite lidded casserole dishes.*

2 littleneck clams
1/4 cup lobster meat, chopped
1/4 cup crab flakes
1/4 cup shrimp
Paprika
4 tablespoons butter, divided
1 tablespoon cooking sherry
1 cup heavy cream, divided
3 egg yolks, slightly beaten
1 tablespoon fresh lemon juice
Salt and pepper to taste

Heat pan or skillet and add two tablespoons of the butter. Sauté clams, lobster, crab flakes, shrimp and paprika for several minutes. Stir in sherry and cook a few minutes more. Add 3/4 cup of the cream and bring to a boil, stirring constantly.

In a small bowl, add the remaining 1/4 cup of cream and the egg yolks and whisk lightly. Add to seafood mixture and continue to stir until thickened. (Do not allow the mixture to boil at this point unless you want to end up with a really fancy omelet.) Remove from heat. Add lemon juice, salt, pepper and the remaining 2 tablespoons of butter. Yields 2 servings.

The Frederick & Nelson tea room is pictured circa 1909. Opposite, the store is shown on a 1924 postcard.

The Frederick & Nelson Store
Seattle, Washington

Frederick & Nelson
Seattle, Washington

Nothing earns a shopper's loyalty quite like receiving excellent customer service, and the Frederick & Nelson department store gave its customers some extraordinary service during the floods of December 1933.

Roads all over Puget Sound were flooded. Roads were impassable. And Christmas gifts had yet to be delivered to some local customers.

Did they get an e-mail informing them the gifts would be delayed? Did they get a robocall informing them Junior's Christmas present was no longer available? Not on your life.

The industrious employees of Frederick & Nelson got in their delivery trucks and transported gifts as far as they could. Then they hopped in their rowboats, paddled through the city and delivered all 425 of those Christmas gifts, God bless us, every one.

Store founder Donald Edward Frederick grew up the son of a plantation owner in Marshallville, Georgia and went west to pursue his fortune.

While working in the gold mines of Colorado, Frederick met Nels B. Nelson of Sweden. Once in Seattle, Frederick went into the used furniture business. When his business partner left, Frederick and his old mining pal Nelson joined forces in the business that would carry both their names. Chinook Indians were some of their first customers.

Like many of the great merchant princes, Frederick and Nelson were growth-minded businessmen. In 1891 they bought another furniture store and began selling new furniture. With the Alaskan gold rush soon underway, Seattle was a boom town so it was the perfect time for a new business to flourish.

The store added departments besides furniture to meet customers' needs, developing into what we now know as a department store.

Other stores influenced the formation of Frederick & Nelson. Robert Spector in his book *More Than a Store* writes that "Frederick had already been influenced by the great retailers of Atlanta such as M. Rich and Bros., which later became the famous Rich's department store. Nelson, who had lived in Chicago, admired that city's Marshall Field & Company, which became a model for Frederick & Nelson."

Nelson died at sea in 1907, leaving his friend to grow the business alone.

Frederick started looking for a new place to build, and the structure known as "Frederick's Folly" went up. It had six stories and a basement, and the forward-thinking Frederick had made sure the foundation was strong enough to eventually hold 10 stories.

The new store had 9-1/2 acres of space, with features including a beauty salon, motion picture auditorium, medical facility, children's nursery, and even reading and writing rooms where weary patrons could get some rest. It also had a tea room.

More Than a Store says "the large, elaborately furnished Tearoom, which could seat 400 and included three private dining rooms, quickly became Seattle's most sophisticated place for lunch. Fashion shows were staged every Wednesday at noon during the fashion seasons, and twice a year the Store featured a special showing of Paris originals."

A popular dessert created by the store's food operation was the Frango frozen dessert. Later the name Frango was given to some chocolate candies made at the store.

Some say the name was an acronym for the store itself: FRederick And Nelson COmpany, with "Franco" later changed to "Frango" to avoid having the same name as the Spanish dictator who met with Hitler. Another theory says "Frango" was a combination of the words "Frederick" and "tango," a popular dance when the candies were first made.

Frederick decided to retire in 1929 and sold his store to Marshall Field for about $6 million. The store continued to be operated as a Seattle store and had almost no staff changes immediately following the sale.

Frederick & Nelson, Seattle's top department store in the 1950s, closed its doors in 1992, and the building is now home to Nordstrom.

Fond memories of the old store remain, and in 1998 the *Seattle Times* responded to a reader request by tracking down a recipe for the store's chicken salad.

Frederick & Nelson's Chicken Salad

There seem to be as many chicken salad recipes as there are tea rooms, and I enjoy trying new ones. This chicken salad gets its unique taste from the addition of black olives.

1 pound boneless, skinless chicken breasts
2 ribs celery, finely diced
1/2 cup chopped pecans
1/3 cup drained, sliced black olives
1 cup mayonnaise
1/4 teaspoon salt
Freshly ground black pepper to taste
1-1/2 teaspoons Worcestershire sauce
1 tablespoon lemon juice

Place chicken breasts in pan, cover with water and bring to a boil. Reduce heat and simmer, partly covered, about 12 minutes more or until the chicken tests done. Remove from pan.

When chicken has cooled, dice and pour into a mixing bowl. Add the celery to the chicken. Reserve a tablespoon of the pecans and two tablespoons of olive slices for garnish, then add the remaining pecans and olives to the chicken.

In separate bowl, mix mayonnaise, salt, pepper, Worcestershire sauce and lemon juice. Add to chicken mixture and combine well. Cover and refrigerate until serving time. Garnish with reserved pecans and olives. Yields 6-8 servings.

Gimbels in New York is shown circa 1951. Its tea room, opposite, once served as a meeting place for soldiers returning from World War I in 1918.

Gimbels
New York, N.Y.

I n my city, there's a car dealership by the name of SouthTowne whose energetic owner regularly appears on TV saying that "Nobody and I mean nobody can beat a SouthTowne deal!"

Whether this local car man knows it or not, he is channeling his inner Bernice Fitz-Gibbon.

Back in the early 1920s, Bernice left the family farm in Wisconsin and went to work in retail advertising at a time when few women did. She and her team wrote advertising copy for everything from blankets and stoves to crabapple trees and canaries, low-priced fabrics and high-priced fashions. Stores smart enough to hire her over the years included some of the biggest names in retailing: Marshall Field, Wanamaker's, Macy's and Gimbels.

It was at Gimbels, in 1945, that Bernice coined the slogan "Nobody but nobody undersells Gimbels." The store was in the middle of a price war, and the boss came by and said he wanted some ad copy fast. Bernice needed to catch a plane to Milwaukee in three hours, so she assured Fred Gimbel she'd have something to him before she left, a headline he could run across every advertising page until she got back in a week.

"My goose is cooked," she thought.

Bernice knew the point of the ad had to be that "nobody undersells Gimbels," but that wasn't catchy. She remembered a line from an A.A. Milne poem she'd read to her children, "The King's Breakfast." The word "nobody" was repeated three times, and Bernice said to herself "nobody, nobody, nobody." Too long. Then she thought of the "nobody but nobody" line. Perfect!

Bernice made her flight that day, and she also made retail history. In her book *Macys, Gimbels, and Me*, she tells of the time Winston Churchill was visiting New York and a dinner was given in his honor. Churchill turned to the guests and asked, "Is it true that nobody, but nobody, undersells Gimbels?"

The Gimbels store in New York was well-known for its long-running (and mostly good-natured) feud with archrival Macy's, but the store actually began as a trading post on the Wabash River in Indiana. Adam Gimbel, a Bavarian immigrant, opened his trading post and advertised "Fairness and Equality of All Patrons, whether they be Residents of the City, Plainsmen, Traders or Indians." He eventually expanded, opening stores in Milwaukee and Philadelphia. The New York store came to life in 1910, a block from Macy's store on Herald Square. In 1923 Gimbels acquired the store we now know as Saks Fifth Avenue.

Gimbels garnered great publicity through the years, whether it was from Fitz-Gibbon's award-winning ads, the banner sales years during the thirties, or the goodwill that came to both Gimbels and Macy's from the 1947 film *Miracle on 34th Street*. In the film, Kris Kringle is hired to perform as the Macy's Santa, but he turns heads by directing Christmas-shopping mothers to other stores if Macy's doesn't have what their child wants. He sends one mother to Gimbels for skates for her daughter.

Gimbels was also featured as a shopping destination for Lucy Ricardo and Ethel Mertz in TV's *I Love Lucy*.

Do you suppose Lucy and Ethel ever dined in the Gimbels Tea Room? Plenty of others did. From the day it opened in 1910, with 125 vases of cut flowers on the tables, Gimbels Tea Room served as a meeting place.

In 1918, Gimbels placed an ad in the *New York Tribune* announcing the store would serve as "Soldiers' and Sailors' Reunion Headquarters" with a comfort station set up in one of the rooms. There, "the boys" and their friends would be able to leave word about where and when to meet and how to locate them.

"A cordial welcome is extended to all military men and women and their families and friends to make this their reunion headquarters. Located in Gimbels Tea Room, 8th floor," the ad said.

The store closed in 1987, and the building is now home of the Manhattan Mall. Perhaps Gimbels will live on in the hearts—or at least the stomachs —of those who try this Gimbels Potato Salad, a frequently-requested dish of former patrons. With a nice crunch from diced celery and a heap of hearty potatoes and eggs, nobody but nobody can find a classier potato salad!

Gimbels Potato Salad

This Gimbels Potato Salad recipe has been mentioned so often on "reader request" websites, I can only assume this was a favorite dish of shoppers dining at Gimbels. After trying it myself, I can see why!

16 small red potatoes
2 cups mayonnaise
8 green onions, chopped
2 ribs celery, finely minced
1 (2-ounce) jar pimiento pieces
8 hardboiled eggs, chopped

Cook potatoes in boiling water until done. Cool in cold water, then peel and slice. In a large mixing bowl, combine mayonnaise, onions, celery and pimientos. Mix well. Add potatoes and eggs and mix gently. Chill. Yields 10-12 servings.

Hess's
Allentown, Pennsylvania

For star power alone, not many stores can claim the drawing power of Hess's in Allentown, Pennsylvania. Zsa Zsa Gabor, Johnny Carson, Troy Donahue, Rock Hudson, Sophia Loren, Lassie and even Superman, George Reeves, were among the celebrities who came to Hess's. Not bad for two businessmen who started their business in the storeroom of a hotel!

Charles and Max Hess were German immigrant brothers who operated a store in New Jersey. In 1896 Max was in Pennsylvania for a volunteer fireman's convention when he saw a location on Hamilton Street in Allentown that he thought would make a good branch location. The next year the brothers opened in Allentown, eventually doing so well they sold the New Jersey store to focus on the Pennsylvania one.

Max Hess Jr. became president in the early 1930s and thus began one of the great chapters in retail history. Hess's motto for the store was "Be the first, be the best, and above all be entertaining."

Who wouldn't be entertained by a store whose owner flew staff all over the world to get the scoop on fashion? Elsa Schiaparelli's first lingerie show in North America was at Hess's. Local women dreamed of owning a gown from Hess's elite French Room, for the store's elegant specialty shop was known for its quality fashions. One longtime customer described Hess's as "the Neiman Marcus of the East."

Max Hess Jr. was not above a little showmanship. While other stores had Santa pull up in a sleigh, Hess's Santa parachuted in from a helicopter. When the store began its popular flower show in 1961, flowers were even hanging from the store's massive crystal chandeliers. When the store sponsored a Trip of a Lifetime contest, they sent one lucky shopper on a European vacation and had the good sense to milk it for publicity with daily articles in the local newspaper.

In department store dining history, Hess's has earned a spot for one especially famous dessert: the Patio Restaurant's Mile High Strawberry Pie.

Irwin Greenberg, a former president and CEO of Hess's, tells about the famous pie in the PBS documentary *Hollywood on Hamilton: Remembering Hess's*.

Strawberries for the pies were flown in from all over the world. The mound of glaze-sweetened berries was topped with a mountain of whipped cream stabilized to hold its shape. Each pie was eight inches high and weighed 10 pounds. Customers ate 10-20 of them each day.

And one of the pie's greatest fans was Liberace.

Mr. Showmanship himself fell in love with the pies and began ordering them for friends as Christmas gifts. Each year, he would order between 50 and 100 pies and have them shipped to friends all over the country.

Although Hess's closed a year shy of its 100th birthday, and the building was later torn down, the store, the legend and the pie live on. In 2000, an Allentown woman took top honors when she competed with 20 others to see who could make the best recreation of the famous pie.

In spring of 2011, students at Brandywine Heights High School in Pennsylvania staged a fashion show in which student waitresses wore dresses featuring the iconic red, green and blue Hess's logo and served the equally iconic strawberry pie.

One wistful 18-year-old summed it up for a lot of Pennsylvania residents when she said, "I wish the store would still be open."

Hess-inspired Strawberry Pie

After several false starts, I was delighted to make a successful (if smaller) version of the famous Hess's Strawberry Pie. My blog readers, who had encouraged me through the flops, cheered. The background paper in the photos is vintage Hess's gift box lining paper found online. I'd love to have a Hess's restaurant plate, bowl or cup-and-saucer set, but those pieces often sell for $100 and up. If you ever come across something with the Hess's logo on it, grab it!

1-1/2 cups + 2 tablespoons sugar
1-1/2 cups water
4 tablespoons corn starch
1 (3-ounce) box strawberry Jell-O
1-1/2 quarts fresh Driscoll's strawberries (or the biggest ones you can find)
1 baked Pillsbury deep-dish pie crust
1 pint heavy whipping cream

In a medium saucepan, whisk together the 1-1/2 cups sugar, water and corn starch over medium-high heat until mixture thickens, about 5 minutes or as long as it takes to get a nice thick texture. Stir in package of strawberry Jell-O and mix well. Remove from heat for a few minutes, then chill mixture in refrigerator until cooled but not set.

While mixture chills, clean and hull strawberries. Use a sharp knife to remove the hulls with the tiniest cuts you can possibly make. Fold strawberries into the gelatin mixture and toss gently with a rubber spatula until every strawberry is covered. Mound mixture into baked crust and pat it down with your hands as firmly as you can without crushing the berries. Refrigerate until set, overnight if possible. When time to serve, pour whipping cream and the 2 tablespoons sugar into a chilled bowl and beat with electric mixer until thickened. Garnish pie with whipped cream as desired.

THE HIGBEE COMPANY "ONE OF THE WORLD'S GREAT STORES", TERMINAL GROUP, PUBLIC SQUARE, CLEVELAND.

The Higbee Company
Cleveland, Ohio

Anyone who's seen the 1983 movie A Christmas Story *knows the tale of little Ralphie and his manic quest for the Red Ryder BB gun he sees in a local department store's Christmas window. It's the one his mother doesn't want him to have because, as she tells him, "You'll shoot your eye out."*

Determined to have the BB gun of his dreams, Ralphie pays a visit to the store's Santa Claus, and even the big guy himself tries to discourage Ralphie from acquiring the gun.

"You'll shoot your eye out, kid," he says. "Merry Christmas!"

The department store display window where Ralphie's BB gun dreams first came to life was at the Higbee Company.

The store was founded in 1860 and changed locations and owners several times over the years. By the 1920s Higbee's was growing so rapidly it had to add two more sales floors. Photographer Margaret Bourke-White began her career in Cleveland after graduating from Cornell, and the store hired her to photograph its display windows.

The famous display window Ralphie peered into was in the now-famous 1931 Higbee building. It opened that year as part of the Terminal Tower development and was connected to the new Cleveland Union Terminal. Twelve stories tall and boasting 1 million feet of floor space, Higbee's was the largest store to open in this country in 20 years. No wonder the little Ralphies of Cleveland wanted to shop there at Christmas!

The Higbee tea room, later to be named The Silver Grille, opened in September of 1931. The early menu offered a soup and salad luncheon for $1, a salad plate for 65 cents and a tea plate for 35 cents. The tea plate consisted of assorted sandwiches, little cakes, and coffee, tea or hot chocolate. On the busiest days, the tea room would serve up to a thousand customers.

Most fortunately for Higbee fans, The Silver Grille and many of its recipes have been well-preserved in two books, *The Silver Grille* (2000) and *The Higbee Company and The Silver Grille* (2001), both by Richard E. Karberg with Judith Karberg and Jane Hazen.

Karberg says The Silver Grille "was designed in the art moderne style, sometimes also called 'steamship modern,'" since it was often used in the design of ocean liners of the late twenties and early thirties.

Karberg describes The Silver Grille decor: "The tables and chairs were made of aluminum by General Fireproofing of Youngstown, Ohio. The table tops, originally black in color, were an early use of Formica. The china, designed to complement the architecture of the room, was supervised by Guy Cowan, who had once operated the famed Cowan Pottery in Rocky River and then worked for Syracuse China in Syracuse, New York. Table linens also echoed the art deco design of the room."

The Higbee Company survived the Depression and performed well as a locally-owned department store chain until the early 1980s. Although the store and tea room are now closed, The Silver Grille is actually one of the few department store tea rooms which may still, at least in a sense, be visited today. It was protected under a Historic Building Tax Credits Program given to the Higbee Building, and in 2002 Forest City Enterprises restored The Silver Grille, including much of the original furniture. With catering provided by the Ritz-Carlton, The Silver Grille is now a special events facility that can, once again, accommodate guests in this historic and beautiful space.

Higbee Cinnamon Muffins

The plain versions of these muffins were served as a bread choice at The Silver Grille, but I liked the crunch of the cinnamon sugar on top of these spiced ones. The recipe is adapted from the book The Higbee Company and The Silver Grille. *A Higbee plate from Syracuse China, below, features the same design that once was used as a border along the tea room's ceiling.*

3/4 cup shortening
1 cup sugar
3 eggs, separated
4 cups flour
1 teaspoon salt
2 tablespoons baking powder
1 teaspoon cinnamon
2 cups milk

Topping:

1/2 teaspoon cinnamon mixed with
3 tablespoons sugar

Preheat oven to 400 degrees. Cream shortening, sugar and egg yolks. In large bowl, combine flour, salt, baking powder and cinnamon. Add shortening mixture to flour mixture alternately with the milk, using a rubber spatula to combine just until well-blended. Gently fold in lightly beaten egg whites. Divide batter into 24 muffin tins prepared with cooking spray. Sprinkle the cinnamon sugar atop the batter and bake for about 17-20 minutes. Yields 24 muffins.

THE J. L. HUDSON COMPANY
Detroit, Michigan

The Mezzanine Tea Room

New Vegetable Soup 15
Cream of Chicken Soup 15
Chilled Orange and Grapefruit Juice 15
Fresh Fruit Cocktail 20

A la Carte Suggestions

Roast Loin of Pork with Buttered New Corn and
Waldorf Nut Salad .75

Orange, Banana, Plum, Grapes and Melon Salad 75

Assorted New Vegetable Plate 75

Individual Chicken Pie with Fricassee Gravy 75

Walnut Muffin, Poppy Seed, French or
Parker House Roll

Tea, Cup of Coffee or Milk

Today's Luncheon Seventy-five Cents

New Vegetable Soup or
Chilled Orange and Grapefruit Juice

Chicken and Ham a la King on Toast or
Fillet of Fresh Perch with Picillili,
Harvard Beets or
Cabbage, Carrot, Cucumber and
Apple Salad with Potato Chips

Pineapple Angel Food Ice Box Loaf with
Foamy Sauce or
Vanilla Ice Cream

Walnut Muffin, Poppy Seed, French or
Parker House Roll

Tea, Cup of Coffee or Milk

Sandwiches
Made with Mayonnaise

White Bread with Bacon and Tomato 40
Whole Wheat Bread with Sliced Ham and Cheese . . .40
Rye Bread with Sliced Liverwurst and
Russian Dressing .25
Banana Bread with Cream Cheese and Jelly 50

Desserts

Old Fashioned Fresh Strawberry Short Cake with
Whipped Cream .40
Baked Peach Roly Poly with Hard and
Supreme Sauce .20
Chocolate Frosted Sponge Butter Cream
Six Layer Cake .20
Pineapple Angel Food Ice Box Loaf with
Foamy Sauce .15
Fresh Strawberry Boston Whipped Cream Pie 20
Mixed Fruit Tart a la Mode 35
Apple Pie 15   a la Mode 30

Fruits

Cantaloupe 25   Chilled Honey Dew Melon .50
Iced Watermelon . . .25   Fresh Strawberries, Cream .50

Ice Creams and Sundaes

Pineapple Sherbet 20   Fresh Strawberry Sundae .25
Vanilla Ice Cream 20   Hot Butterscotch Sundae .20
Chocolate Ice Cream .20   Fresh Fruit Sundae 25
Strawberry Ice Cream .20   Hot Fudge Nut Sundae . .25
Orange Pineapple Ice Cream .20   Chocolate Sundae .20

Beverages

Cup of Coffee 10   Pot of Tea 15
Cup of Postum 10   Buttermilk 10
Golden Jersey Milk . .10   Chocolate Milk 15
Milk Shake 15   Coca Cola 10
Glass of Iced Tea 10   Chocolate Malted Milk .20
Pineapple Mint Soda . .20   Root Beer Boston Cooler .25

Prices subject to 3% State Sales Tax   *July 12, 1947*

Detroit's Police Department asks everyone's help in its traffic safety program, *"Watch Out For Kids"*

J. L. Hudson Co.
Detroit, Michigan

O nly one department store ever helped found an automobile company, and perhaps only Motor City in its heyday could have supported a larger-than-life store such as J. L. Hudson. Its founder was, at first glance, such an unlikely candidate for success in either retailing or auto making.

Joseph Lowthian Hudson was born in England in 1846 to a father, Richard Hudson, who was a part-time Methodist preacher and a small tea, coffee and spice merchant. The family moved to Canada and then Michigan, where young Joseph held jobs ranging from telegraph operator to sales clerk and fruit picker.

He and his father opened a small general store, and then the Panic of 1873 hit. The father died. The son tried to salvage what remained, but he eventually filed for bankruptcy, settling with creditors for 60 cents on the dollar. He started over as an employee in another store.

By 1888, Hudson owned an even bigger store in Detroit. "Even more remarkable," according to *The Great Merchants*, "he looked up all the creditors whose claims had been erased by the bankruptcy proceedings and paid them in full with compound interest. Such action is rare. ... it astounded the business world. The amazed creditors showered him with gifts and praise."

Hudson shortly moved into an eight-story building at Farmer and Gratiot Streets, but friends thought the location was too far uptown and the store couldn't possibly succeed. It did. Hudson added on to his building, and in 1911 he constructed a 10-story addition on Woodward Avenue.

With his nephews helping run the store, Hudson now had time for other activities, such as serving as a partner and financial backer for the Hudson Motor Car Company. Some 4,000 cars were sold the first year of production.

On Hudson's death in 1912 his nephews, the Webber brothers, took charge. By 1945 they had started on an addition which made Hudson's a full block square. Everything about this store was big. The store once claimed it stocked 553,921 items from A to Z, from anti-macassars to zippers, aspirin to zwieback, an African mask to Zuercher cheese. Departments in the store were home to Detroit's biggest bookstore, biggest drugstore and biggest toy store. At one time the store boasted the biggest private switchboard in Michigan, and only the Pentagon's was larger.

Another of the store's most memorable "biggest" features was the U.S. flag which once hung on the side of the building. Dedicated in 1949 and added on to over the years, the 104 x 235-foot flag was seven stories tall, weighed about 1,500 pounds, and took 55 individuals to display.

There was little you couldn't find at Hudson's. If you needed travel arrangements, typing lessons, a haircut, a shoeshine, a pharmacist or even help planning a home, Hudson's had it.

To fuel the busy shoppers who came their way, the store's Foods Division offered choices including a basement cafeteria, the Mezzanine Tea Room and Mezzanine Soda Fountain. Formal dining rooms included the Georgian Dining Room, the Early American Dining Room and the Pine Room.

The July 12, 1947 Mezzanine Tea Room menu listed the day's luncheon special. For 75 cents a customer could get New Vegetable Soup or Chilled Orange and Grapefruit Juice; Chicken and Ham a la King on Toast or Fillet of Fresh Perch with

Picillilli; Harvard Beets or Cabbage, Carrot, Cucumber and Apple Salad with Potato Chips; Pineapple Angel Food Icebox Loaf with Foamy Sauce or Vanilla Ice Cream; Walnut Muffin, Poppy Seed, French or Parker House Roll; and Tea, Cup of Coffee or Milk. Whew!

The *Detroit News* says the store's restaurants made 14,000 meals a day, and "the Hudson's Maurice salad delighted lunchers for many years, its recipe a closely guarded secret until the store bowed to thousands of requests and made it public."

And that basement cafeteria? In 1960 Hudson's decided to reach out to the growing minority community and hired its first black bus girl. An aspiring singer, she hadn't yet achieved superstar status and needed a job to tide her over.

So, do you think Diana Ross ever ate a Maurice Salad? Think it o-o-ver.

Hudson's Maurice Salad

Though I was sorry to learn the Hudson's building was imploded in 1998, I'm grateful to have been introduced to Hudson's Maurice Salad, known for its creamy dressing made with onion juice. You can find bottled onion juice online, but it's easy to acquire your own. Simply cut off the root end of the onion and scrape it with the back of a spoon. The juice will easily dribble down along with some of the pulp.

Dressing:

2 teaspoons white vinegar
1-1/2 teaspoons lemon juice
1-1/2 teaspoons onion juice
1-1/2 teaspoons sugar
1-1/2 teaspoons prepared Dijon mustard
1/4 teaspoon dry mustard
1 cup mayonnaise
2 tablespoons fresh parsley, chopped fine
1 hardboiled egg, diced
Salt to taste

Salad:

1 head Iceberg lettuce, shredded
8 ounces ham, cut into strips
8 ounces turkey breast, cut into strips
8 ounces Swiss cheese, cut into strips
1/2 cup miniature Gherkin pickles
8–12 green olives with pimientos

Combine vinegar, lemon juice, onion juice, sugar and mustards and mix well. Add remaining dressing ingredients and blend. Divide lettuce among plates and top with strips of ham, turkey and cheese. Add pickles and garnish each salad with 2 olives. Top with dressing. Yields 4 meal-size salads or 6 smaller salads.

Innes Block, Wichita, Kans.

Innes Department Store
Wichita, Kansas

O ne of today's best mergers of old-fashioned cooking and newfangled technology comes in the form of websites devoted to vintage recipes.

Wichita's Innes Department Store was known for a favorite cream pie once served in the store's tea room. The proprietress of RecipeCurio.com scanned the recipe for Innes' Rum Cream Pie, which was "clipped from a newspaper and found in a large collection, date unknown."

One of the charming things about this recipe is that it hails from a midwestern department store that probably isn't as widely known as a Marshall Field or Wanamaker's.

Walter Pease Innes got his start when, at 24, he bought the old McNamara store whose owner had just died. Most department stores were named for one or more of the founders, but this dry goods company was originally called the Geo. Innes Co. in honor of Walter's uncle and financial backer, George Innes.

In 1907 Walter Innes caused a stir in the business community by designing a big new store and locating it two blocks away from the center of the town's retail world.

The Innes store's tea room was a popular meeting spot for local groups. Local printers held an evening banquet there in 1921, and the Alpha Chi Omega girls had a luncheon there in 1922. The Traffic Club of Wichita installed officers at an Innes Tea Room dinner in 1936.

The tea room also got good reviews along the way. The famous food critic Duncan Hines—yes, the one whose name appears on cake mix boxes today—wrote about the Innes Tea Room in his 1959 guidebook *Adventures in Good Eating*.

"This department store tea room is one of the most popular and best-liked in Wichita," Hines said. "Besides the regular dining room there is a Men's Grill. They are proud of the pastries and hot breads made on the premises."

The restaurant was also spotlighted in the December 1961 issue of *Ford Times*, a small digest-sized publication from the Ford Motor Company. Along with the tea room's recipe for Stuffed Ham Rolls with Creamed Chicken, it included this review:

"Although situated in the Innes Department Store at 121 S. Broadway in downtown Wichita, the dining rooms are popular with men as well as women. Among the culinary attractions are hot breads and homemade pastries. Lunch is served in the Men's Grill and tea room from 11:30 a.m. to 2:30 p.m. The dinner hours are from 5:30 to 8:30. Closed on Sunday and holidays."

In early 1962, the *Wichita Eagle* reported on the death of Mrs. Ethel Corrigan, 82, who served as director of the Innes Tea Room from 1924 until her retirement in 1955. She built up clientele from 250 per day to 1,500, the paper said.

In the fifties the store was sold to Younker Brothers, and later to Macy's and then Dillards.

It became the Finney State Office Building in 1994, named in honor of Joan Finney, the state's 42nd governor and its first woman governor.

Innes Tea Room's Rum Cream Pie

Although I do not care for Rum Cake, this Rum Cream Pie was delightful and one of my favorite recipes in this book. That drippy caramel on the bottom? Oh. My. Goodness.

12 Werther's chewy caramel candies
1/2 cup + 3 tablespoons heavy whipping cream, divided use
1-1/2 teaspoons rum flavoring, divided use
1 (9-inch) deep-dish pie shell, baked
1-1/2 cups milk
1/2 cup sugar
5 tablespoons sifted flour
1 tablespoon corn starch
1/4 teaspoon salt
2 eggs, beaten well
1/2 cup heavy whipping cream, whipped with 1 tablespoon sugar
Extra whipped cream for garnish

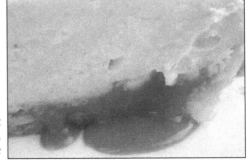

In double boiler over high heat melt candies and the three tablespoons of cream, stirring constantly until combined and the consistency of caramel ice cream topping. Add 1/2 teaspoon of the rum flavoring. Spread caramel mixture over bottom of baked and cooled pie shell.

In double boiler over medium heat, heat the milk and 1/2 cup of cream. Mix sugar, flour, corn starch and salt and add to hot milk mixture in double boiler. Stir until thickened, about 15 minutes. Whisk about 1 cup of the hot mixture into the beaten eggs, then stir egg mixture into the milk and cream and cook 2 or 3 minutes more, stirring constantly. Let cool completely. Add remaining 1 teaspoon of rum flavoring, fold in the whipped cream and blend well before pouring into pie shell. Chill in refrigerator until set. Garnish with more whipped cream if desired. Yields 8-10 servings.

F. & R. Lazarus
Columbus, Ohio

L ast-minute Christmas shoppers everywhere, let us now pay homage to the great F. & R. Lazarus department store in Columbus, Ohio. If it weren't for a member of this store's founding family, the always-hectic Christmas shopping season might be even shorter than it already is!

Simon Lazarus founded the first Lazarus store in 1851, and he was also the first rabbi of Temple Israel, the oldest Jewish congregation in Columbus. The store grew with the help of Lazarus' wife and sons Fred and Ralph, but it was grandson Fred Lazarus Jr. who would bring the F. & R. Lazarus store to its glory days, and we can be thankful for that.

In fact, we even have Fred Lazarus Jr. to thank for the fact Thanksgiving now falls on the fourth Thursday each November.

In June of 1939 Fred Jr. was at a dinner meeting with other merchants when he observed that Thanksgiving fell on the last day of the month that year. If it could be moved up a week, Fred said, merchants would have six more days in the Christmas retail season.

There was nothing to prevent changing the date of Thanksgiving, which had in fact been celebrated on many different days. The idea for the earlier observance gained traction, and some fans of the idea presented it to President Franklin D.

Roosevelt. It took a few years to find its way into law, but in 1941 Congress decreed Thanksgiving would now fall on the fourth Thursday in November. That meant the holiday would never be later than Nov. 28, although it can fall as early as Nov. 22.

On behalf of last-minute shoppers everywhere, thank you, Mr. Lazarus.

Fred Jr. was also known for his great belief in the retailer serving as a showman. "A good store is like a big circus," he said. "You can have one ring, or five or twenty. That is why a department store has it all over others in attracting people to come in and look around."

Perhaps that explains such store attractions as the live alligator in the basement and the "tooting whistle" system of store weather forecasts. (One toot: Fair. Two toots: Rain. Three toots: Unsettled.)

The store was also influential in the history of American retailing as a founding partner of the Federated Department Stores group.

Lazarus was known for introducing a "Secret Gift Shop" where children could shop "alone" supervised by employees. While children shopped, adults had the option of dining in one of several different restaurants at the store, which over the years included The Chintz Room, The Buckeye Room, The Copper Kettle and the Rose Fountain.

An article by Bart Mills in the *Lima News* noted Lazarus "was one of the first department stores to experiment with adding food service to its lineup. In the early 1880s, the company added a 25-seat soda fountain to its downtown Columbus store. A century later, the chain had expanded with its food service division."

The downtown Columbus store closed in 2004 following a buyout by Macy's. The Columbus Downtown Development Corp. has since restored the building and turned it into "green" office space, for which it won a 2010 preservation award from Columbus Landmarks.

Fortunately for its fans, Lazarus also preserved, and published, some of its most-requested restaurant recipes, including such favorites as Lazarus Cheesecake, Lazarus House Dressing, several cream soups, and even a sweet bread made with spinach leaves and an orange.

The *Lima News* said recipes have been published in at least three soft-bound books and are available over the internet, so "the restaurants may be gone, but the memories can live on through the food."

Cream of Cauliflower & Cheese Soup

Bless the Lazarus Department Stores for thoughtfully compiling a booklet of restaurant recipes. Cream soups always make me think of classic tea room fare, and this Cream of Cauliflower & Cheese Soup is elegant and oh-so-easy to prepare. Have some in homage to the man and the store who made sure we'd always have plenty of days to Christmas shop each year!

2 cups cauliflower florets, chopped into 1/2-inch pieces
1/2 cup water
1 stick (4 ounces) unsalted butter
1/2 cup all-purpose flour, sifted
2 cups chicken stock
4 ounces cheddar cheese, shredded
2 cups half-and-half
1/2 teaspoon salt
Dash of white pepper

Using a small saucepan, steam cauliflower in the 1/2 cup water over low heat. Do not drain. In another pan, melt butter over low heat. Add flour and stir constantly for about 3 minutes. Add chicken stock and stir with a wire whisk. Bring to a boil, stirring constantly. Then lower heat before adding cauliflower, cheese, half-and-half and seasonings. Yields 4 large servings, more if served in smaller amounts in teacups or cream soup bowls.

R. H. Macy Company, New York, N. Y.

K 9143

"It's smart to be thrifty" appears below the name Macy's on this vintage postcard. The slogan was coined by the great advertising woman Bernice Fitz-Gibbon. Opposite is a Macy's Tea Room menu from 1929.

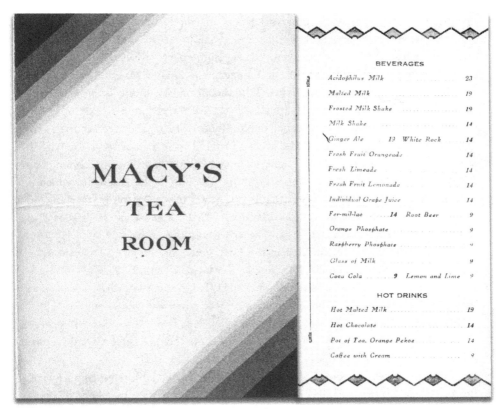

MACY'S
TEA
ROOM

BEVERAGES

Acidophilus Milk		23
Malted Milk		19
Frosted Milk Shake		19
Milk Shake		14
Ginger Ale	13 White Rock	14
Fresh Fruit Orangeade		14
Fresh Limeade		14
Fresh Fruit Lemonade		14
Individual Grape Juice		14
Fer-mil-lac	14 Root Beer	9
Orange Phosphate		9
Raspberry Phosphate		9
Glass of Milk		9
Coca Cola	9 Lemon and Lime	9

HOT DRINKS

Hot Malted Milk	19
Hot Chocolate	14
Pot of Tea, Orange Pekoe	14
Coffee with Cream	9

R. H. Macy & Co.
New York, N.Y.

I n retailing, a chain's primary or best-known store is sometimes referred to as the "flagship" store. It's a particularly fitting term for Macy's legendary Herald Square store, since Macy's iconic red star is based on the tattoo Macy's founder got as a teen when he worked on a whaling ship.

Rowland Hussey Macy was born into a Quaker household on Nantucket Island, Massachusetts and headed to sea at 15. After four years on the whaling ship, Macy went home before going to work for a printer in Boston. After several failed attempts to open a retail business, Macy tried again with a store in New York at 6th Avenue and 14th Street. The sign overhead read "R.H. Macy, Dealer in Dry Goods," and at 36 his determination paid off.

When the store was just a few years old, Macy hired Margaret Getchell, a former schoolteacher and his distant cousin, to work at the store. Getchell became the first American woman executive in retailing.

In the 1870s, Macy was approached by a young man, Nathan Straus, who hoped the store would carry his family's china and glassware. The Straus family leased a space in the basement, and the line proved very profitable for Macy's. The Straus and Macy families became close friends, and a decade or so after Macy's death Nathan and his brother Isidor became partners in the firm. Under the Strauses Macy's expanded and built the store that still stands at 34th Street today.

The Herald Square Macy's opened in November of 1902, and the *New York Times'* complimentary review spoke of the food service: "The restaurant is in the eighth story, and it has the advantages of light, air, and a fine outlook. It can accommodate 2,500 persons. There is a forty-ton absorption machine in the basement, which is used for refrigerating and cooling the drinking water to a temperature of about 40 degrees. By means of the thirty-three elevators and the four escalators, it is easy to move the shoppers from one story to another without overcrowding."

Macy's isn't usually mentioned in the same breath as some of the stores more well-known for their tea rooms—Wanamaker's, Marshall Field, Bullock's Wilshire— but a 1929 menu titled "Macy's Tea Room" shows that it, too, took advantage of what writer Jan Whitaker called "the tea room craze" that swept the country in the 1920s.

Offerings included a Cream Cheese, Jelly and Nut Bread Sandwich (23 cents), slices of Lemon Meringue Pie and Brownies (14 cents each), Raspberry and Orange Phosphates (9 cents) and a pot of Orange Pekoe tea (14 cents).

Speaking of tea, one bit of Macy's lore may be of particular interest to tea lovers. Books on tea history usually credit New York tea and coffee merchant Thomas Sullivan with creating the tea bag. Sullivan was giving his customers pre-measured packets of loose tea tied in silken pouches, and when customers began dunking the pouches themselves, the tea bag was born, or so the story goes.

Macy's has an alternative theory of the tea bag's invention. Robert Grippo's book *Macy's* has a profile of William Titon, Macy's Wine and Food buyer. Grippo says William Titon's daughter "proudly tells the story of another of her dad's ground-breaking ideas. For years, Macy's sold some of the finest teas in the world. Some time before World War One—the exact year has been lost over time—a gentleman offered loose tea for Titon's consideration. When the leaves accidentally spilled onto the tasting room floor, Titon gathered them into one of his linen handkerchiefs and decided to brew the tea within the cloth rather than dumping it loose into the pot. Thus was born the tea bag, which Macy's proudly sold."

And Macy's has "proudly sold" quite a few things in its 153 years of business. In 2011, the trade journal *Stores* magazine cited Macy's, with its 848 stores, as the top-selling department store in the country.

Macy's 1932 Cookbook Brownies

Mabel Claire wrote cookbooks "For the Busy Woman" that were sold in department stores such as Macy's. I've fudged a bit by including this recipe since I don't know this is the exact brownie served in Macy's tea room. However, the period is correct and this brownie was certainly Macy's-endorsed! Claire's advice to women is fun to read, like this tidbit in The Macy's Cook Book: *"The kitchen should be the pleasantest room in the house. There is no good reason for the millions of ugly kitchens in the world. Nor is there any good reason for kitchens that look like white tile lunchrooms. In a kitchen that is gay, cozy and pleasant, half the labor of cooking seems to be eliminated." Ponder that while you bake these tasty, fudgy brownies.*

2 eggs
1–1/4 cups brown sugar
1/2 teaspoon vanilla
1/2 cup flour
2 squares unsweetened Baker's chocolate, melted
1/3 cup walnuts, chopped

Preheat oven to 350 degrees. Beat eggs well and add sugar. Add remaining ingredients and combine. Spread evenly in a buttered 8 x 8-inch pan and bake for 20 minutes.

12434 MAISON BLANCHE, NEW ORLEANS, LA.   DETROIT PUBLISHING CO.

The 12-story Maison Blanche store shown at left was the tallest building in New Orleans until 1921. The older store, with its domes and turrets, is shown opposite.

Maison Blanche
New Orleans, Louisiana

Jingle, Jangle, Jingle, here comes Mr. Bingle
With another message from Kris Kringle
Time to launch the Christmas season
Maison Blanche makes Christmas pleasin' ...

Ever heard of Mr. Bingle? If you were a child growing up in New Orleans you certainly did.

The legend goes that a snowman appeared near Santa Claus' sleigh one day and Santa took him on as a helper. After Santa touched him, the snowman could walk and talk, and Santa gave him a pair of holly wings so he could fly. Santa even gave him some ornaments for eyes. The little fellow was completely hatless, however, so Santa gave him an ice cream cone for a hat, along with a magical candy cane.

For years, the hope of seeing Mr. Bingle brought children and their parents to the store on Canal Street.

Maison Blanche, which means "White House" in French, was opened in 1897 by a German immigrant, Isidore Newman. The original building, located on the edge of the French Quarter, was soon replaced by a 12-story building that was the city's tallest until 1921. (Today it's a Ritz-Carlton Hotel.)

Newman's family ran the store until it was sold to City Stores in 1951, and later to the Sternberg family. The Sternbergs were merchants from Baton Rouge and owners of Goudchaux's, at one time the largest family-owned department store in America.

A 1960 luncheon menu from The Rendezvous restaurant at Maison Blanche included some fairly typical offerings—such as Tuna Fish Salad, Sliced Elberta Peaches with Cottage Cheese on Crisp Lettuce, and a Hawaiian Fruit Plate—but also local specialties such as Shrimp Remoulade and Fried Fresh Lake Pontchartrain Shrimp. The Shopper's Special, consisting of Breaded Choice Pork Chop, Red Beans and Steamed Rice, Hot Roll and Butter, was 65 cents.

But at Christmastime no store attraction was more popular than seeing Mr. Bingle at one of the 15-minute puppet shows he starred in each day. Mr. Bingle—who cleverly shared the same initials as Maison Blanche—was the creation of Emile Alline, the store's display director, and puppeteer Edwin "Oscar" Isentrout.

Hans Sternberg wrote a book, *We Were Merchants*, about how his parents fled Nazi Germany and came to America and opened Goudchaux's. When the store bought Maison Blanche, they also got Mr. Bingle.

"This character was promotional ingenuity at its best," Sternberg said. "Mothers would bring their children to Maison Blanche, leaving the youngsters to have 'Breakfast with Mr. Bingle' while they shopped."

Other department stores had their own special Christmas characters and events just for children.

• Aunt Holly and Uncle Mistletoe were originally display window characters before they became part of the Christmas tradition at Marshall Field in Chicago.

• Priscilla the Pink Pig was both a character and a children's ride at Rich's Department Store in Atlanta.

• Rudi was a popular Christmas bear character at Wanamaker's in the 1980s.

While nostalgia for many of these characters remains, none seems to inspire loyalty quite like Mr. Bingle. He has his own fan page on the internet and his own Facebook page.

If you want some Mr. Bingle memorabilia, save your pennies, for the plush toys fetch considerable amounts at online auctions and retail websites. Ornaments, cards and cookbooks also show up occasionally.

When Dillards became the new owner of Maison Blanche and the Mr. Bingle character, the company donated a giant papier mache figure of Mr. Bingle they inherited to the New Orleans City Park. It was refurbished just in time for the 2005 Christmas season.

Jingle, Jangle, Jingle, here comes Mr. Bingle!

Mr. Bingles

Some of the children who grew up going to Maison Blanche at Christmas have fond memories of eating these Mr. Bingle treats. This recipe is adapted from one in Holly Clegg's now out-of-print cookbook for children, From Mr. Bingle's Kitchen.

5 tablespoons unsalted butter
3 cups miniature marshmallows
1/3 cup creamy peanut butter
4 cups Rice Krispies cereal
6 sugar cones (I used 4-1/2-inch cones with a 2-inch diameter opening)
Assorted round jelly-type candies, sliced in half, to serve as eyes and buttons (I used the sour candy balls from Jelly Belly)
3 multi-colored jelly beans, sliced in half lengthwise
Extra peanut butter to serve as "glue" for attaching features
Cooking spray
Colorful cupcake paper liners

In a large pan over low heat, melt butter. Add marshmallows and stir constantly until combined. Add peanut butter and continue stirring until combined. Remove from heat. Add cereal and stir gently until mixture is thoroughly combined. Let cool for about 5 minutes.

Spray hands with cooking spray and shape mixture into six balls. (Mine were about 2-1/2 inches in diameter.) Make sure balls are well-shaped or the cereal may drift apart. Flatten slightly on bottom. Place balls on wax paper and allow to stand for 30 minutes. Flatten two different colored cupcake papers and sit one cereal ball on top. For hat, spread edge of cone opening with peanut butter and place on top of ball. Use peanut butter to attach round candy "buttons" for decorating hat. Add eyes and mouth in same fashion. Yields 6 Mr. Bingles.

THE NARCISSUS TEA ROOM, SEVENTH FLOOR
ONE OF SIX TEA ROOMS IN THE MAIN STORE

MARSHALL FIELD & COMPANY, RETAIL, CHICAGO

THE SOUTH GRILL ROOM, MARSHALL FIELD & CO., RETAIL, CHICAGO

Marshall Field
Chicago, Illinois

W alking through his Chicago store one day, Marshall Field came upon an assistant retail manager arguing with a woman customer.

Field asked the manager what was going on.

"I am settling a complaint," replied the man.

"No you're not," snapped Field. "Give the lady what she wants!"

The shy farm boy from rural Massachusetts hadn't dedicated his life to business only to watch a customer be mistreated.

Field worked his way up the retail ladder beginning at age 16 when he went to work in a dry goods store. He memorized prices. He studied women's fashions in *Godey's Lady's Book*. And perhaps his

A vintage Marshall Field matchbook cover

THE WALNUT GRILL ROOM, SEVENTH FLOOR
ONE OF SIX TEA ROOMS IN THE MAIN STORE

MARSHALL FIELD & COMPANY, RETAIL, CHICAGO

natural shyness was actually an asset, for young Field learned to listen to the ladies and focused on their needs.

After working as a clerk and then a junior partner, Field became a full partner in Field, Leiter and Company. When the store opened in 1868, ladies were given roses and a feast for their eyes: cashmere shawls, sealskin cloaks, and the finest silks, velvets and furs.

If ever a merchant should have been tempted to hang it up early on, though, it was Field. The Great Fire of 1871 turned the Field and Leiter store into a pile of smoking ruins, but Field found a new site in two days. The delivery horses got distemper in 1872, so the store turned to oxen. And when another fire destroyed their second store in 1877, Field and Leiter again had a new location in just two days.

The partners parted ways in 1881, and the business at State and Washington Streets would simply be known as "Marshall Field and Co."

In addition to "Give the lady what she wants," another store motto might have been "Give the lady what she wants *to eat*," since a tea room had opened by 1890. Field himself had opposed the idea but was persuaded by employee Harry Selfridge, who would one day found his own department store, Selfridge's, in London.

The tea room was on the third floor near furs. On the first day they served 56 customers, but within a year they were serving as many as 1,500 a day.

"Eventually, this tea room became one of several restaurants and dining rooms on the store's seventh floor, some decorated with palms, some filled with heavy oak tables and carved chairs, some with open grills where chops and steaks were broiled in the

This vintage demitasse cup and saucer came from the Marshall Field Tea Room.

sight of the customers, some serving sandwiches in tiny baskets with bows on their handles—all of them catering to thousands of shoppers every day," said Lloyd Wendt and Herman Kogan in their book *Give the Lady What She Wants*.

On New Year's Day 1906, Field played golf in the snow, using red golf balls, with his nephew, a Field's employee, and Robert Todd Lincoln, the surviving

son of President Abraham Lincoln. Field died of pneumonia about two weeks later. A grandson and great-grandson would later serve on the board of directors, but upon Field's death John Shedd became president. He had the store torn down and a new one constructed. One of its greatest features was a dome designed by Louis Comfort Tiffany containing thousands of pieces of Favrile glass, the biggest glass mosaic in existence.

The era of department store tea rooms may have reached its pinnacle with the Marshall Field restaurants, including the Walnut Room, the Narcissus Room, the Wedgwood Room and others.

Though Macy's moved into the flagship store in 2006 and gave it their name, Field's customers were still protesting the change in fall of 2011.

You don't know whether to admire their loyalty or suggest they all meet in the old Walnut Room to enjoy some of the still-available Chicken Pot Pie!

Mrs. Hering's Chicken Pot Pie

Marshall Field legend says a Mrs. Hering was at work in the store's millinery department one day when she heard some customers complaining they had nothing to eat. She offered them some of the homemade chicken pot pie she had brought for lunch. By 1890, a restaurant had opened in the store. You can find a number of versions of this recipe on the internet, but here's the way I made it, adapted from The Marshall Field's Cookbook.

Chicken and stock:

1 (3-1/2 pound) frying chicken
1 carrot
1 celery stalk
1 small onion, cut in half
2 teaspoons salt

Crust:

1-1/2 cups all-purpose flour
1/2 teaspoon salt
1/2 cup unsalted butter, chilled and cut into 1/2-inch cubes
1/4 cup vegetable shortening, chilled
3 to 4 tablespoons ice water

Filling:

6 tablespoons unsalted butter
1 large onion, diced (about 1-1/4 cups)

3 carrots, thinly sliced on the diagonal
3 celery stalks, thinly sliced on the diagonal
1/2 cup all-purpose flour
1-1/2 cups milk
1 teaspoon fresh thyme leaves, chopped
3/4 cup frozen green peas, thawed
2 tablespoons minced fresh parsley
2 teaspoons salt
1/2 teaspoon freshly ground black pepper

Combine chicken, carrot, celery, onion and salt in a large pot. Cover with cold water and bring to a boil. Reduce heat and simmer for 45 minutes. Remove chicken from pot and let cool for 15 minutes. While chicken cools, continue to boil the remaining water and vegetables. Once chicken has cooled, strip away as much meat as you can, place on a dish and set aside. Return bones to the stockpot and continue to boil for about 15-20 minutes more. Strain and set aside 2-1/2 cups of stock. Remaining stock can be used for another purpose. (Discard vegetables.)

For crust, combine flour and salt in a food processor. Add cold butter and pulse to combine. Add shortening and pulse a few more times until dough is consistency of coarse cornmeal, with some pea-sized pieces of butter. Slowly add ice water by the tablespoon, pulsing after each addition, until the dough sticks together. Place the dough on a clean surface and mold into a ball, then flatten. Sprinkle with a little flour, wrap with plastic wrap, and refrigerate for at least 30 minutes.

For filling, preheat oven to 400 degrees. In a large pan, melt butter and add onions, carrots and celery. Cook until onions are translucent, about 10 minutes. Add flour and stir, cooking for one minute more. Whisk in the 2-1/2 cups of stock. Whisk in milk. Decrease heat to low and simmer for 10 minutes, stirring often. Add chicken, thyme, peas, parsley, salt and pepper and stir. Divide the filling among six 10-ounce ramekins.

For crust, roll out dough on a lightly floured surface to about a quarter-inch thick. Cut into 6 rounds, slightly larger than the circumference of the ramekins. Place a dough round on top of each pot pie filling. Fold excess dough under itself. Cut a 1-inch vent into each pie. Place ramekins on baking sheet and cook for 25 minutes or until the pastry begins to brown. Yields 6 servings.

A mural was featured on a wall of the English Tea Room at Miller & Rhoads.

MILLER & RHOADS THE SHOPPING CENTER RICHMOND, VIRGINIA

Miller & Rhoads
Richmond, Virginia

Of all the department stores a tea-room-loving time traveler could wish to visit, Miller & Rhoads in Richmond, Virginia would have to top the list for many reasons.

Are you a fan of vintage hats? At Miller & Rhoads you can visit The Amethyst Room and have their legendary hat designer, Sara Sue Sherrill, embellish your chapeau and polish it off with a label reading "Designed for you by Sara Sue."

Love old dishes? You will have a treat in store at the Miller & Rhoads china department, where elegant displays of the finest patterns stretch as far as the eye can see.

Perhaps you're a book lover? Plan early to get a ticket for the store's first Book and Author dinner, where the featured guest is Betty Smith, author of *A Tree Grows in Brooklyn*. If you prefer to skip the dinner, just visit the book department another day when Pearl Bailey or Mrs. Woodrow Wilson is visiting. (Try to get there a little early for Miss Bailey, though. She was so popular the original shoppers kept her there past closing time!)

Whichever type of retail activity lures you into the store, you'll want to take the elevator up to the fifth floor and visit the Miller & Rhoads tea room. A vintage menu reveals that if you happen to visit on June 8, 1929, here's what one dollar will get you: Fruit Cup or Chilled Consomme, Cream of Celery, Fried Chicken with Pastries,

Buttered Corn, Broiled Tomato or Soft Shell Crabs on Toast, Tartar Sauce, Green Peas, Asparagus Tips, Poinsetta (sic) Salad, Mayonnaise Dressing, Pineapple Parfait or Raspberries with Ice Cream or Caramel Meringue Tarts or Choice of Ice Cream. Orange Pekoe Tea will cost you another 10 cents, so plan accordingly.

And if, by chance, you're one of those for whom the favorite holiday is Christmas, you'll probably want to wait until December to visit, for as everyone in Richmond knows, the real Santa is always at Miller & Rhoads!

Virginia's Miller & Rhoads was started in 1885 by three Pennsylvanians who decided they wanted to go into the dry goods business in the South. One of the three left after a few years, leaving Linton Miller and Webster Rhoads as partners.

Earle Dunford and George Bryson wrote a book titled *Under the Clock: The Story of Miller & Rhoads* that includes store history and vintage photos which give the flavor of a beloved retailer. They show Richmond when Broad Street was still traveled by horse and by trolley; a store display window promoting war bonds during WWII; the elegant Amethyst Room where Sara Sue worked her magic; Santa and the store's Snow Queen visiting with the governor; and a window commemorating Jamestown's 350th anniversary.

The Miller & Rhoads tea room figures prominently in the store's history. In addition to hosting hungry shoppers, the tea room was the site of business lunches, special fashion shows, and the store's famed Book and Author Dinners.

Fashion designer Gloria Vanderbilt dined at the store and so enjoyed the Chocolate Silk Pie that she persuaded store management to give her the "secret recipe" which, mercifully, is not so secret anymore.

The tea room stayed open through Jan. 12, 1990, even though the store had closed to shoppers on Jan. 6, but the building still exists today. It's now the home of a Hilton Garden Inn which says it "combines historic charm with modern amenities."

Yes, but can you still get a slice of that Chocolate Silk Pie?

Miller & Rhoads Chocolate Silk Pie

Crust:

1/2 cup unsalted butter
1/2 cup granulated
sugar
2 cups graham cracker
crumbs

Filling:

1/2 cup unsalted butter
3/4 cup confectioners'
sugar
1 ounce unsweetened
baking chocolate, melt-
ed according to package
directions and cooled
Pinch of salt
1 teaspoon vanilla
extract
3 pasteurized eggs
(since this filling is uncooked, it is important to use only pasteurized eggs)

Garnish:

2 cups heavy whipping cream
2 tablespoons confectioners' sugar
Chocolate Jimmies

Chill a 9-inch regular pie plate in your refrigerator or freezer. Preheat oven to 350 degrees.

Using electric mixer, beat butter and granulated sugar until light and fluffy. Slowly add just enough graham cracker crumbs to make a slightly crumbly mixture. Press evenly into pie plate and cook for 5 minutes. Let cool while you prepare the pie filling.

With electric mixer, beat butter and confectioners' sugar until light and fluffy. Add melted chocolate, salt and vanilla. Add one egg and—this is very important!—beat for no less than 5 min-utes. Add second egg and beat for no less than 5 minutes. Add third egg and beat for no less than 5 minutes. Pour filling into cooled pie shell and refrigerate for 24 hours.

Before serving, prepare whipped cream by adding confectioners' sugar to the heavy whip-ping cream and beating with electric mixer until soft peaks form. Pipe or spread onto top of pie and garnish with chocolate Jimmies.

The flagship Neiman Marcus store in Dallas, shown here on a vintage postcard, is still serving shoppers today.

Neiman Marcus
Dallas, Texas

Sure, the president of Neiman Marcus called her "the Balenciaga of food." And yes, President Lyndon Johnson tried to hire her to come cook for him at the White House. Even so, all you really need to know about Helen Corbitt can be learned from the plaque that once hung in her kitchen. It read:

This is the kitchen of Helen Corbitt.
I Am The Boss!
If you don't believe it ...
Start something!

Before Giada, before Ina, before Rachael and Nigella, there was another cooking celebrity whose Texas-sized personality would have put those amateurs to shame. Some called her "the Julia Child of Texas," which is rather amusing when you consider she was actually from New York.

The legendary Helen Corbitt is best remembered for her role as Director of Food Services for Neiman Marcus, though it took Stanley Marcus eight years to lure her there. But what Marcus wanted, Marcus usually got.

You can still visit one of the store's cafés today and be served Helen's famous hot-from-the-oven popovers and strawberry butter.

Helen was born in New York but became sufficiently Texan that when the *Houston Chronicle* named its "100 Tallest Texans" of the century in 2000, the legendary Corbitt made the list alongside President Lyndon B. Johnson, George Foreman, Howard Hughes, Buddy Holly and, yes, her old boss, Stanley Marcus.

After graduating from Skidmore College, Helen worked in New York as a hospital dietitian. Not content with dietetics, she looked for another job and the only one she could find was teaching large quantity cooking and tea room management in Austin, Texas. Once, directed to prepare a convention dinner using only Texas products, which didn't exactly excite her, Helen mixed garlic, onion, vinegar, oil and black-eyed peas and called it "Texas Caviar." (Neiman Marcus later canned it, and customers ordered it by the case.) Helen also worked at the Houston Country Club, the tea room at Joske's department store in Houston, and the Driskill Hotel in Austin before she finally decided to go to work for Stanley Marcus.

In her book *The Best from Helen Corbitt's Kitchens*, editor Patty Vineyard MacDonald tells how celebrities often came to dine at the store, including Carol Burnett, Princess Margaret, Bob Hope—even Moses (Charlton Heston). A memorable visitor at the Zodiac Room was opera diva Maria Callas, who MacDonald writes, "made a luncheon reservation for her party of thirty. Renowned for keeping everyone waiting, she was over a half-hour late, so Corbitt instructed the staff to break down the long table and serve people who had been waiting patiently in line. Callas's retinue swept in still later and were consigned to the end of that long line."

The store whose restaurants Corbitt made famous, Neiman Marcus, got its start in Texas in 1907. Partners Herbert Marcus, his sister, Carrie Marcus Neiman, and her husband, Al Neiman, originally went to Atlanta, Georgia to start a sales promotion business. They were so successful they were offered the opportunity to sell out by taking a franchise in an upstart soft drink company. The partners declined to go into business with Coca-Cola (say, anyone know what ever happened to them?) and returned to Dallas to open a store.

Herbert's son Stanley Marcus liked to joke that the store was founded on a poor business judgment.

Retail historians note that Neiman Marcus is really a "specialty" store and not a true department store. While it is organized by department, those departments focus on style and fashion and tend not to include the more mundane offerings such as everyday furnishings and TV sets.

Neiman Marcus is known for its high-end luxury goods, with well-publicized Christmas catalogs offering everything from His and Her airplanes to a recreation of Noah's Ark and a Monopoly game crafted entirely of chocolate.

The store's personal service was legendary, and that extended to customers whether the purchase was large or small. In his book *Minding the Store*, Stanley Marcus recounts one memorable Christmas Eve when he got a frantic phone call from a customer 200 miles away who had ordered 24 $5 gifts to be gift-wrapped and serve as table decorations and place cards. "The gifts had arrived," Marcus said, "but they were not gift-wrapped as specified, and as a result her whole Christmas dinner table decor was ruined. It was then two-thirty, and her party was to start at six-thirty. I told her not to worry, for I would charter a plane and send a gift-wrapper to her home. Our specialist was there by five o'clock, wrapped the presents, placed them on the table, and went out the back door as the guests started coming in for dinner."

It was that level of above-and-beyond service that always meant so much to the store's customers.

Of course, if that hostess had really wanted to impress her guests, she would have asked them to send over Helen Corbitt to prepare the meal!

Neiman Marcus Popovers with Strawberry Butter

It's rare that I have occasion to stop by the Zodiac Café at Neiman Marcus in Atlanta, but when I do, I like to order one of their wonderful salmon salads preceded by the traditional demitasse cup of consommé and some Neiman Marcus Popovers with Strawberry Butter.

1 cup sifted all-purpose flour
1/4 teaspoon salt
2 eggs
7/8 cup milk
1 tablespoon melted butter

Preheat oven to 450 degrees. Mix the flour and salt. Beat eggs until light, add milk and butter, and add slowly to the flour. Stir until well blended. Beat 1 minute with electric mixer. Heavily butter popover pan (unless using a non-stick pan) and put it in the oven to heat. When hot, fill cups to one-third with batter. Bake 20 minutes at 450 degrees, then reduce heat to 350 degrees and bake 15 minutes more. Don't peek! Serve hot with strawberry butter. Yields about a dozen mini-popovers.

Strawberry Butter

1 cup butter, softened
1 cup strawberry preserves (I used the seedless variety)

Blend well and store in refrigerator.

In September of 1950, Rich's Magnolia Room displayed 40 American paintings from the famed Holbrook Collection at the University of Georgia. (Photo courtesy of Kenan Research Center at the Atlanta History Center)

Rich's
Atlanta, Georgia

Gloria Swanson of Sunset Boulevard *fame staged a fashion show here. Bob Hope and Marjorie Kinnan Rawlings autographed books here. And when the* Gone With the Wind *cast reunited for the 50th anniversary of the movie in 1989, they did so right here, at the downtown Atlanta Rich's store. And to think, the founder came to this country in steerage!*

This vintage postcard from 1967 reads: "Every Thanksgiving Evening, in a traditional finale to a day spent with family and friends, all Atlanta and vicinity usher in the Christmas season with the lighting of the 'Great Tree' on RICH's Crystal Bridge." Opposite, the store is shown on a 1947 postcard.

FORSYTH STREET • *Showing Great New* **RICH'S**
The Largest and Most Modern Department Store in the whole Great South

Morris Rich may have arrived in this country under the humblest of circumstances, but unlike poor Leonardo DiCaprio's character Jack in the movie *Titanic*, Rich made the journey safely and had many great years ahead of him.

Rich was born in Hungary in 1847, the same year the Georgia town of Marthasville changed its name to Atlanta. As a young boy, Morris joined his older brother William on a ship bound for New York. Some of their friends from the old country had settled in Cleveland, so the Rich brothers sought them out and soon found jobs and boarding in the town.

After the Civil War the brothers struck out on their own, William to Atlanta and Morris to Chattanooga, Tennessee. Soon Morris gave up on Chattanooga and went to Georgia as well, working as a pack peddler and selling goods door to door. In 1867, he decided to make Atlanta his home. Borrowing $500 from his brother, Morris opened a little store on Whitehall Street, today known as Peachtree Street.

One of Georgia's most beloved journalists, Celestine Sibley, in 1967 wrote a book celebrating the store's centennial titled *Dear Store: An Affectionate Portrait of Rich's*. In it, she shared stories of the many citizens who became faithful customers of the store. When the price of cotton fell in the twenties, Rich's offered to buy 5,000 bales at more than the market price. During the Depression, a Rich's executive read that the Atlanta schools were too broke to make payroll for the teachers. He suggested they be paid in scrip, a type of credit, which Rich's cashed at full value—and the teachers weren't obligated to spend a penny of it at the store.

Sarah, Duchess of York, above left, was at the North Point Mall Rich's in 1999 to promote Wedgwood china (photo courtesy of *The Newnan Times-Herald*). At left and above, the original Rich's clock still keeps time on the old store downtown, which closed in 1991 and is now part of the Sam Nunn Federal Building.

Sibley wrote of the time in 1945 when "war-weary troops arrived at Fort McPherson one Saturday afternoon before Labor Day, ready to be discharged on Sunday morning. It was a time of rejoicing for the men and their families, except for one little detail. The Army's vault was time-locked for the weekend and they couldn't get their pay until Tuesday. Rich's promptly opened up its safe and advanced the money for the payroll."

Like other department stores of its era, the downtown Atlanta Rich's store had a popular eating and meeting spot in its Magnolia Room. A Rich's booklet from the store's 75th anniversary in 1942 noted that "Rich's Tea Room, its two soda fountains and Employes' (sic) Cafeteria utilize twelve and three-quarter tons of food a week ... serve between 3,500 and 4,000 meals a day ... 18,000 COCA-COLAS and 9,000 cups of COFFEE a week." The tea room was also listed as the meeting place for such groups as the Credit Men, Christian Council and Atlanta Council PTA, along with 20 private parties a week, four fashion shows each Tuesday and autographing teas.

One of the more colorful events staged in the Magnolia Room was the annual tea party held for Rich's customers 80 and older. In May of 1950, some 300 guests 80-and-older attended, including 23 who were 90 or older. Among the guests was 104-year-old W.J. Bush of Fitzgerald, Georgia's only surviving Confederate veteran.

And the Magnolia Room is a place still fondly remembered by women in the Atlanta area today.

One patron, Ruth Schroeder, grew up on an island in Maine where she had no access to any restaurant at all, much less a tea room. When she moved to Georgia, she enjoyed taking her young daughter to the Rich's tea room.

"I felt so elegant," Schroeder said, adding that she wanted her daughter to learn about the finer things in life she never had access to while growing up.

Louise Davis remembers visiting the tea room with a friend in the 1970s. The two women would drive to an outlying MARTA station and take the train into the city to dine at the Magnolia Room. Davis said her regular fare included chicken salad, cheese straws and pot pie, but she also remembers how delicious the water was. She inquired about the source of this great tasting water and learned it came straight out of the tap from the City of Atlanta!

The Magnolia Room is also meaningful to Cynda Pierce, who remembers going there with her mother. Pierce had been a tea room customer for years by the time she first took her 9-month-old daughter, who was still nursing and didn't yet eat much table food.

Pierce had taken a break to stop off and discreetly nurse her daughter before going to the tea room, but the baby wasn't hungry then. By the time they got to the Magnolia Room and the food arrived, Pierce said, "she was quite fussy and constantly reached for my plate. I was at my wit's end because I didn't want her to become a nuisance to the other diners, but she was getting louder and louder. The waitress stopped by the table and suggested that I order something for her. When I explained

Members of the cast of *Gone With the Wind* gathered at the downtown Atlanta Rich's store in 1989 to celebrate the 50th anniversary of the movie. From left are Patrick Curtis, Greg Giese, Evelyn Keyes, Butterfly McQueen, Ann Rutherford, Rand Brooks and Fred Crane, partially hidden, and Cammie King Conlon. (Photo by Winston Skinner and courtesy of *The Newnan Times-Herald*)

that she didn't usually get table food, the waitress suggested that I try a grilled cheese sandwich and cut it in very tiny bites. I reluctantly agreed 'knowing' my baby wouldn't eat it. Not only did she eat every bite, but she also sucked the middle out of some of the french fries that came with it. My daughter's very first table meal was at the Magnolia Room!"

Rich's would eventually become Rich's-Macy's, and in 2005 the Rich's name disappeared entirely. The store and its tea room are both gone now, but a fondness for the food remains. Fortunately for those who ate at the Magnolia Room, some of its best-loved recipes have been preserved in local cookbooks and articles in Atlanta newspapers and magazines. Today anyone can recreate such popular dishes as the Chicken Salad Amandine and Frozen Fruit Salad, a culinary tribute to the cherished Atlanta department store which left its mark upon the South.

Rich's Magnolia Room Frozen Fruit Salad

Years ago I went to a church newcomers' brunch where the food was especially delightful. The hostesses had made copies of all the recipes and had them available at each dish. I loved the frozen fruit salad, and it was only once I got home that I realized this delicious treat was Rich's Magnolia Room Frozen Fruit Salad.

    1 (8-ounce) package cream cheese, softened
    1/2 cup confectioners' sugar
    1/3 cup mayonnaise
    2 teaspoons vanilla extract (I used clear)
    1 (8-3/4-ounce) can sliced peaches, well-drained
    1 (6-ounce) jar maraschino cherries, well-drained and sliced into halves
    1 (30-ounce) can fruit cocktail, well-drained
    1 (8-ounce) can crushed pineapple, well-drained
    2 cups miniature marshmallows
    1/2 cup heavy whipping cream, whipped
    Red or yellow food coloring, optional (I used two drops of red to get a soft, pale pink)

In bowl of electric mixer, cream the cream cheese and confectioners' sugar on medium speed. Add mayonnaise and blend, then add vanilla extract. Remove bowl from mixing stand and use a rubber spatula to fold in fruit and marshmallows. Gently fold the whipped cream into fruit mixture. Add food coloring if desired. Line a muffin pan with paper baking cups and use an ice cream scoop to fill them with the frozen fruit salad. Freeze immediately for at least 3 hours. Remove 15 minutes before serving, but do not allow salads to get soft. Remove baking cups or muffin liners before serving. Yields 12 fruit salads.

Rich's Magnolia Room Chicken Salad Amandine

This recipe is based on one that appeared in the Atlanta newspaper a few years ago, except that I halved it, since I don't typically need 12 servings of chicken salad, and substituted boneless chicken breasts for the bone-in variety. If you require more servings, it's easy to double the recipe.

3 large boneless chicken breasts
3 ribs celery, diced
1/4 cup pickle relish (I used sweet pickle relish)
3/4 teaspoon white pepper
1 cup mayonnaise
1/4 cup sliced almonds, toasted

Boil chicken breasts in water for about 20 minutes, and reserve stock for another use. When chicken has cooled, cut into medium-size strips. Combine celery, pickle relish, pepper and mayonnaise. Fold chicken into mayonnaise mixture. Cover and refrigerate until serving time. Just before serving, garnish with almond slices. Yields 6 servings.

Rich's Magnolia Room Cheese Straws

These aren't your traditional cheese straws, but they are incredibly delicious. If you can serve them hot out of the oven, do so! There's nothing like that light, flaky crunch of freshly baked puff pastry oozing with cheesy goodness. The recipe comes from the book I Rode the Pink Pig, *a tribute to the Rich's Christmas character Priscilla the Pink Pig.*

2 cups grated Cheddar cheese
1/3 cup grated Parmesan cheese
1 teaspoon cayenne pepper, or to taste
Dash of kosher salt
1 (17.3-ounce) box puff pastry, 2 sheets
2 tablespoons butter, softened

Preheat oven to 425 degrees and lightly spray a cookie sheet with cooking spray. Mix cheeses, pepper and salt. Spread one puff pastry sheet with butter. Spread with cheese mixture. Place second pastry sheet on top. Press together ends of pastry. With a rolling pin, roll out to 1/4-inch thickness, about 15-by-15 inches. Cut across in 1-inch wide ribbons. Cut in half again. Twist each piece. Bake for 3 to 5 minutes or until puffed and lightly browned. Yields about 30 cheese straws.

Rich's Magnolia Room Pecan Cream Torte

This recipe for Rich's Pecan Cream Torte is an old Magnolia Room recipe I found in a vintage Atlanta cookbook. If you like the crunch of our famous Georgia pecans and the rich sweetness of freshly whipped cream, this is a cake you don't want to miss!

1-1/2 cups light brown sugar
1 cup cake crumbs (I used slices of pound cake from the grocery store bakery, lightly toasted and pulsed in a food processor)
1/2 cup shortening
2 tablespoons all-purpose flour
1/2 teaspoon baking powder
5 large eggs, separated
2 cups pecans, finely chopped (divided use)
1 pint heavy whipping cream
1 tablespoon sugar

Preheat oven to 350 degrees. Grease and flour two 9-inch cake pans and line them with wax paper.

Using a stand mixer, cream brown sugar, cake crumbs, shortening, flour and baking powder until smooth and creamy. Add 5 egg yolks and 1-1/2 cups of the pecans. Mix until smooth.

In a separate bowl, whip the five egg whites until they reach the soft peak stage, then fold them into the batter. Divide batter equally among the pans and bake for 25-35 minutes until firm. Do not overbake. Let cake cool completely, then whip the heavy whipping cream with 1 tablespoon sugar. Place first layer on cake plate, add generous layer of frosting, then place second layer on top and frost entire cake. Garnish sides of cake with remaining pecans.

JOHN WANAMAKER BUILDING, PHILADELPHIA, PA.

John Wanamaker
Philadelphia, Pennsylvania

"Have only the best mince pies that money will buy. Even if you have to sell at a loss. I can afford to sink $10,000 a year in mince pies rather than have people say I do not give them good pies. The people of Philadelphia can't be fooled on mince pies."

– John Wanamaker, to his restaurant manager

J ohn Wanamaker of Philadelphia was one of the first merchants to open a restaurant in his store. Apparently he was also one of the first to discover such restaurants often operate at a loss. Yet Wanamaker knew that having customers eat in his store was simply a smart way to keep them there—and keep them shopping— even longer.

An 1889 article in the Altamont, New York newspaper *The Enterprise* heaped praise on the Wanamaker dining enterprise:

"John Wanamaker has one of the biggest kitchens in the world. It is in the basement of his Philadelphia store, where no rats are tolerated and no dampness is permitted to penetrate. Wanamaker takes great pride in this kitchen, as he does in everything connected with his store. Often he goes down to the big steam cooking pans, lifts the lid, tastes the soup, peeps at boiling potatoes, or inspects the little porcelain pan in which the charlotte russo is served. Wanamaker is noted for his rich charlotte russo, and the delicacy is made from a recipe furnished the chief cook by Wanamaker himself. Wanamaker likes to take visitors through his kitchen and ask them to sample the food in all its stages of preparation. His is one of the few great kitchens in the world which a man may go through and come out with a good appetite. ... In Wanamaker's

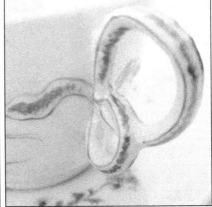

This bow-handled teacup and saucer set is stamped GDA France, John Wanamaker.

restaurant, from 4,000 to 8,000 persons are fed every day, and Wanamaker is not too proud to lunch in his own shop."

Wanamaker went into business with his brother-in-law in 1861, opening a store in Philadelphia on the eve of the Civil War. His brother-in-law died just seven years later. Wanamaker opened another store, and soon the two businesses were doing so well he purchased the old Pennsylvania Railroad freight depot to turn it into a store. The Grand Depot, as it was now called, also included a restaurant.

In addition to being a savvy businessman, Wanamaker was well-known for his faith and his community service. A devout Presbyterian, he wouldn't even so much as advertise on Sundays. He was active in Sunday School, the YMCA and politics, serving President Benjamin Harrison as postmaster general.

In 1902, an aging store and competition from other merchants caused Wanamaker to think about new plans for his flagship store. (He also had a store in New York by this time.) The Philadelphia store was rebuilt in stages so business could continue as usual. The new Wanamaker store was dedicated on Dec. 30, 1911, with President William Howard Taft attending, and that morning Wanamaker was honored at a surprise breakfast in the store's Great Crystal Tea Room.

And what an elegant tea room this was! The largest dining room in Philadelphia, it was 22,000 square feet and could accommodate 1,400 diners. According to a book the store published in its Jubilee year, the woodwork was oak, with a Circassian brown finish, with white walls and floors of oak parquetry. Decor was generally Renaissance in style, modeled after the tea room in the home of Robert Morris, a financier of the American Revolution.

The Great Crystal Tea Room took its name from the impressive lighting system in which a large number of glass reflecting electroliers brilliantly reflected light from all the hanging crystals in the room.

Two other important features exclusive to the new store both came from the 1904 St. Louis Exposition: a 2,500-pound bronze eagle and the exposition organ. The eagle would become a popular meeting place for Wanamaker shoppers, and the store's concerts featuring the world-famous Wanamaker Organ were legendary.

They still are, for that matter. Today the store is operated as Macy's Center City, and Macy's notes that the Wanamaker Grand Court Organ now has nearly 28,500 pipes and is "the largest playable instrument in the world." It is also a National Historic Landmark.

Concerts are still performed twice each day, Monday through Saturday.

And perhaps some kind Philadelphian can even tell you where to get a good mince pie.

Crystal Tea Room Hot Cheese Tarts

This recipe appeared in The Philadelphia Cook Book of Town and Country *and is attributed to the John Wanamaker Crystal Tea Room. The plain cheese tarts are delicious, and this recipe could easily be varied by adding diced vegetables or small amounts of breakfast/brunch meats.*

4 eggs, beaten
1 cup heavy whipping cream
1 cup milk
8 ounces Swiss cheese, grated
Pinch of paprika
Salt to taste (I added pepper as well)
Pastry for tart shells (I used frozen pie crusts from the grocery store)

Preheat oven to 450 degrees. Remove prepared pie crusts from pan, roll out on wax paper and cut circles from the pastry using a 3-inch round cookie cutter or glass. Line the cups of a 12-tart pan with the rounds. (I use Nordic Ware's tart pan, but if I didn't have it I would simply use mini-muffin pans, adjusting the size of the pastries as needed.) Combine eggs with whipping cream, milk and cheese. Add seasoning to taste. Mix well and fill tart shells. Bake for 10-12 minutes or until tarts are just starting to brown on top. Yields about 1-1/2 dozen 2-inch cheese tarts.

Tea rooms for both children and adults are shown on these vintage postcards from Woodward & Lothrop department store.

Woodward & Lothrop
Washington, D.C.

~ⓒ~

W hen you think of Washington, D.C.'s Woodward & Lothrop Department Store, the one thing you need to remember is this: Play-Doh.

Carpet manufacturers across the country should certainly wish to remember the store, for it was there the popular children's modeling clay was first sold.

Originally invented as a wallpaper cleaner, Play-Doh—which at first came only in off-white—wasn't yet a household name when it was first demonstrated at Woodward & Lothrop's toy department in 1956. Inventor Joe McVicker re-released his product as a children's toy and became a millionaire by age 27.

Woodie's, as Woodward & Lothrop was known to the locals, was about more than just Play-Doh, though. For many years it and Hecht's reigned as the capital's top two department stores.

Samuel Walter Woodward and Alvin Mason Lothrop were dry goods merchants in Massachusetts before they opened their department store at 11th and F Streets NW in Washington, D.C. in 1887.

Like most other department stores, Woodward & Lothrop expanded into the suburbs after World War II, but the family-owned business was determined to grow slowly rather than be swallowed up by another chain. It remained a part of downtown Washington until 1995.

The families were also active in D.C. life. Woodward was president of the Washington City YMCA, and his daughter Helen and her husband donated most of their Bethesda, Maryland estate to form the National Institutes of Health.

In addition to the political movers and shakers who came through the doors of Woodward & Lothrop, the store was also a popular shopping spot for young ladies attending Bryn Mawr, Stephens, Vassar, Radcliffe and Mount Holyoke.

That may be one reason a Woodward & Lothrop Tea Room menu from 1935 lists a variety of delectable offerings including, for 20 cents, a slice of Wellesley Fudge Cake.

The popular chocolate treat is said to date to the 1880s. Two Wellesley College graduates found the recipe in a Boston newspaper and began making it for the Wellesley Tea Room. The classic recipe uses Baker's chocolate, which has been around since 1780 and has been famous ever since.

Take a bite of Wellesley Fudge Cake and you'll see why!

Wellesley Fudge Cake

This may be one of the best chocolate cakes I've ever baked. When I took the leftovers to the office they disappeared quickly, and I received lots of compliments, especially on the rich, chocolatey frosting.

4 (1-ounce) squares unsweetened Baker's chocolate
1/2 cup water
1-3/4 cups sugar, divided use
1-2/3 cups all-purpose flour
1 teaspoon baking soda
1 teaspoon salt
1/2 cup butter
3 eggs
3/4 cup milk
1 teaspoon vanilla

Frosting:

4 squares unsweetened Baker's chocolate
2 tablespoons butter
1 (16-ounce) box of confectioners' sugar
Dash of salt
1/2 cup milk
1 teaspoon vanilla

Preheat oven to 350 degrees. Grease and flour two 9-inch round pans. In small saucepan, heat water, chocolate and 1/2 cup sugar, stirring constantly, for 2 minutes. Remove from heat and cool to lukewarm. Mix flour, soda and salt in a separate bowl.

Cream butter and remaining 1-1/4 cups sugar until light and fluffy. Add eggs one at a time, beating thoroughly after each addition. Add half of flour mixture and beat until smooth. Add milk and remaining flour mixture alternately in two parts. Beat after each addition. Add vanilla and chocolate mixture. Blend well. Divide batter among pans. Bake for 30 to 35 minutes or until a toothpick inserted into the cake comes out clean.

For frosting, melt chocolate with butter over very low heat, stirring constantly until smooth. Remove from heat. Combine sugar, salt, milk and vanilla. Add chocolate, blending well. If necessary, let stand until frosting thickens, stirring occasionally. Spread quickly, adding a small amount of milk if frosting thickens too much. Yields enough frosting to cover tops and sides of two 8- or 9-inch layers, the top and sides of one 9-inch-square or 13 x 9-inch cake or 24 cupcakes.

A Corner of the Garden Room
YOUNKERS TEA ROOM
Des Moines, Iowa

A 1942 postcard, above and opposite, was written by a child to "Dedde" and reports that "We saw some better escalator than the May." The May was the name of another department store of that day.

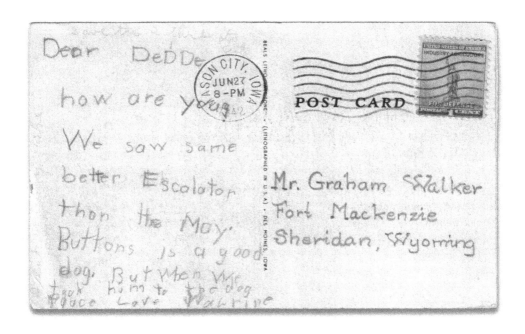

Younker Brothers
Des Moines, Iowa

"But finally there came a day when I was perhaps eight or nine that I was shopping downtown with my mom, with my sister not there, and my mother said to me, 'Shall we go to the Tea Room?' I don't believe I have ever been so eager to accept an invitation. We ascended in an elevator to a floor I didn't even know Younkers had. The Tea Room was the most elegant place I had ever been—like a stateroom from Buckingham Palace magically transported to the Middle West of America. Everything about it was starched and classy and calm. There was light music of a refined nature and the tink of cutlery on china and of ice water carefully poured. I cared nothing for the food, of course. I was waiting only for the moment when I was invited to step up to the toy box and make a selection."

– *Bill Bryson*, The Life and Times of the Thunderbolt Kid

Humorist Bill Bryson was more worried about the toy he would get than in what kind of chicken salad he might be served, but still he manages to capture the atmosphere of going to the tea room at Younker Brothers department store in the fifties.

(Tragically, Bryson's toy box takeaway that day was a *doll*, a gift he tried unsuccessfully to exchange.)

Vintage postcards from the tea room seem to corroborate Bryson's memories: white tablecloths, water goblets, silverware, chandeliers and ruffled curtains.

The store was founded as a dry goods business by Lytton, Samuel and Marcus Younkers in Keokuk, Iowa. Younger brother Herman opened a store in Des Moines, and later the Keokuk store closed and Des Moines became headquarters for the brothers.

In 1912 they purchased the Grand Department Store, and its tea room opened the following year, with a new one replacing it in 1927.

A menu from the 1940s shows tea room offerings ranging from the 65-cent Salad and Sandwich Suggestion (Assorted Fresh Seafood Salad Sandwich on Toast, Potato Chips, and Tea, Coffee or Milk) to the 85-cent Shopper's Luncheon (Escalloped Chicken and Home-Made Noodles, Buttered Green Beans, Peach and Toasted Coconut Salad and Hot Roll).

REFLECTIONS IN *Younkers* TEA ROOM
DES MOINES, IOWA

Where you meet your friends and enjoy good food

By 1943, the store had grown and it was time to purchase the seven-story building across the street, which became the Store for Homes. An underground tunnel connected the two stores, whose unique configuration was duly noted by Bill Bryson in *Thunderbolt Kid*: "It occupied two buildings, separated at ground level by a public alley, making it the only department store I've ever known, possibly the only one in existence, where you could be run over while going from menswear to cosmetics."

Younkers is still in business today as part of Bon-Ton stores. The flagship Des Moines store closed in 2005 and was purchased by a developer in 2008. Plans call for the building to become apartments and commercial and retail space—and to keep the historic tea room.

Younkers Tea Room Chicken Salad

A chicken salad made with sunflower seeds and Ranch salad dressing? I was intrigued when I came across this recipe on several websites mentioning the Younkers Tea Room. I took a bite. Then I was impressed!

3 cups chicken thighs (boiled and broth saved for another use)
1 cup finely diced celery
1/4 cup finely diced onion
1/4 cup roasted, unsalted sunflower seeds
1 cup prepared Ranch salad dressing
1 teaspoon celery salt
1/2 teaspoon dried and minced garlic

Boil chicken thighs, remove chicken from pot and allow the chicken to rest for about 10 minutes. Tear thighs into large pieces and place in food processor, pulsing until chopped but still containing some chunks of the chicken. In a large mixing bowl, combine chicken and remaining ingredients. Toss well, cover and allow flavors to meld in the refrigerator overnight. If you eat this immediately it may taste like it needs some salt and pepper, but try to restrain yourself. Leave this overnight and the flavors of the minced garlic and celery salt really come through the next day. Yields 6 servings—or a heap of tea sandwiches.

Conclusion

❧

In July 2011 *Stores* magazine reported on the top 100 retailers in the country according to retail sales figures. In the number one spot was Walmart, followed by Kroger, Target, Walgreen and Home Depot. The highest-ranked department store in the top 100 was Macy's, which came in at #15. Amazon.com (#19) ranked higher than Nordstrom (#34). Family Dollar (#48) ranked ahead of Neiman Marcus (#81).

We shoppers are a fickle bunch, as downtown department stores learned in the forties and fifties when customers began moving to the suburbs and doing more of their shopping there. Department stores followed the shoppers to the suburbs by building branch stores, but in the last decade or so even those have all but disappeared. We've seen malls turn into "lifestyle centers," and who can even predict how internet sales will influence our shopping in the future!

Did department stores really matter? I am more convinced than ever that they did. If you're a history buff as I am, you might enjoy tracking down a book or two about your old hometown department store and its founders. These men (and some women) were people of great character and determination, often devoted to faith, family and community. I'm intrigued at how often failure marked their early careers. Immigrants who came here with little but the clothes on their backs were proud to become Americans, frequently saving money so other family members could join them in this great land of opportunity. In today's less than flourishing economic climate, it's quite encouraging to read about businesses who survived despite the various financial "panics" they lived through. We aren't the first generation to have to figure out how to earn a living despite economic challenges.

I'd be hard pressed to name a favorite merchant (besides Morris Rich, of course), but I must confess I think retail sainthood should have been bestowed upon Marshall Field the instant he uttered his famous "Give the lady what she wants!" All smart retailers know it's wise to keep their customers happy, but it's worth noting that so many of the early successful merchants turned customer service into an art form.

It's also fortunate that so many of them decided customers needed a place to nourish themselves while out shopping. Department store tea rooms were the right idea at the right time, and oh, do I wish they were still around.

Studying the food of these tea rooms, what impressed me most is how well many of these recipes have aged. We still eat chicken pot pie and cheese straws. Chocolate Silk Pie and Wellesley Fudge Cake are mighty hard to improve upon.

There are many more recipes I plan to try and will write about on the Dainty Dining blog (daintydining.blogspot.com), so I hope you'll visit and share a memory of your own favorite department store, or perhaps a recipe if you've got one tucked away.

Meanwhile, I think I'll go make some chicken salad!

Sources

Appel, Joseph H. *Golden Book of the Wanamaker Stores, Jubilee year 1861-1911*. Philadelphia: John Wanamaker, 1911.

Bryson, Bill. *The Life and Times of the Thunderbolt Kid*. New York: Broadway Books, 2006.

Claire, Mabel. *Macy's Cook Book*. New York: Greenberg, 1932.

Clegg, Holly Berkowitz. *From Mr. Bingle's Kitchen*. Baton Rouge, Louisiana: Maison Blanche, 1987.

Davis, Margaret Leslie. *Bullocks Wilshire*. Los Angeles: Balcony Press, 1996.

Dunford, Earle and George Bryson. *Under the Clock: The Story of Miller & Rhoads*. Charleston: The History Press, 2008.

Fitz-Gibbon, Bernice. *Macy's, Gimbels, and Me*. New York: Simon and Schuster, 1967.

Grippo, Robert M. *Macy's: The Store. The Star. The Story*. Garden City Park, New York: Square One Publishers, 2009.

Hauser, Michael and Marianne Weldon. *Hudson's: Detroit's Legendary Department Store*. Charleston, S.C.: Arcadia Publishing, 2004.

Hendrickson, Robert. *The Grand Emporiums*. New York: Stein and Day, 1979.

Herrick, Elizabeth Webb. *Curious California Customs*. Los Angeles: Pacific Carbon & Printing Co., 1934.

Karberg, Richard E. with Judith Karberg and Jane Hazen. *The Silver Grille*. Cleveland, Ohio: Cleveland Landmarks Press, Inc., 2000.

Karberg, Richard E. with Judith Karberg and Jane Hazen. *The Higbee Company and The Silver Grille*. Cleveland, Ohio: Cleveland Landmarks Press, Inc., 2001.

Levitas, Earlyne S. *Secrets from Atlanta's Best Kitchens*. Charleston, S.C.: Walker, Evans & Cogswell Co., 1971.

Lisicky, Michael J. *Wanamaker's: Meet Me at the Eagle*. Charleston, S.C.: The History Press, 2010.

MacDonald, Patty Vineyard, editor. *The Best from Helen Corbitt's Kitchens*. Denton,

Texas: University of North Texas Press, 2000.

Mahoney, Tom and Leonard Sloane. *The Great Merchants*. New York: Harper and Row, 1974.

Marcus, Stanley. *Minding the Store*. Denton, Texas: University of North Texas Press, 1974.

Morgan, Roberta. *It's Better at Burdines*. Miami: The Pickering Press, 1991.

Reed, Anna Wetherill. *The Philadelphia Cook Book of Town and Country*. New York: Bramhall House, 1963.

Rich's–Macy's. *I Rode the Pink Pig*. Athens, Georgia: Hill Street Press, 2004.

Sibley, Celestine. *Dear Store: An Affectionate Portrait of Rich's*. Atlanta: Peachtree Publishers, Ltd., 1990.

Siegelman, Steve. *The Marshall Field's Cookbook*. San Francisco: Book Kitchen, 2006.

Spector, Robert. *More Than a Store: Frederick & Nelson 1890 to 1990*. Bellevue, Washington: Documentary Book Publishers Corporation, 1990.

Wendt, Lloyd and Herman Kogan. *Give the Lady What She Wants*. South Bend, Indiana: And Books through special arrangement with Marshall Field and Co., 1952.

Whitaker, Jan. *Service and Style*. New York: St. Martin's Press, 2006.

Whitaker, Jan. *Tea at the Blue Lantern Inn: A Social History of the Tea Room Craze in America*. New York: St. Martin's Press, 2002.

Wolcott, Imogene. *The Yankee Cook Book*. New York: Ives Washburn, Inc., 1939.

Newspapers: *Altamont Enterprise, Denver Post, Des Moines Register, Houston Chronicle, Lima News, Los Angeles Times, Miami Herald, Newnan Times-Herald, Reading Eagle, Seattle Times*

Websites: chroniclingamerica.loc.gov, celebrateboston.com, food.com, LostRecipesFound.com, pdxhistory.com, recipecurio.com, westword.com, Wikipedia Commons

---

About the author: Angela Webster McRae is an award-winning journalist and free-lance writer from Newnan, Georgia. She welcomes your own stories and/or recipes from other department store tea rooms. You may write to her at daintydining@gmail.com.

CPSIA information can be obtained
at www.ICGtesting.com
Printed in the USA
JSHW030301070123
35608JS00002B/68

9 780615 533452